ISBN 0-8373-2950-7

C-2950   CAREER EXAMINATION SERIES

This is your
PASSBOOK® for...

Public Information Officer

Test Preparation Study Guide

Questions & Answers

NATIONAL LEARNING CORPORATION

PASSBOOK®

NOTICE

This book is *SOLELY* intended for, is sold *ONLY* to, and its use is *RESTRICTED* to *individual,* bona fide applicants or candidates who qualify by virtue of having seriously filed applications for appropriate license, certificate, professional and/or promotional advancement, higher school matriculation, scholarship, or other legitimate requirements of educational and/or governmental authorities.

This book is *NOT* intended for use, class instruction, tutoring, training, duplication, copying, reprinting, excerption, or adaptation, etc., by:

(1) Other Publishers

(2) Proprietors and/or Instructors of "Coaching" and/or Preparatory Courses

(3) Personnel and/or Training Divisions of commercial, industrial, and governmental organizations

(4) Schools, colleges, or universities and/or their departments and staffs, including teachers and other personnel

(5) Testing Agencies or Bureaus

(6) Study groups which seek by the purchase of a single volume to copy and/or duplicate and/or adapt this material for use by the group as a whole without having purchased individual volumes for each of the members of the group

(7) Et al.

Such persons would be in violation of appropriate Federal and State statutes.

PROVISION OF LICENSING AGREEMENTS. — Recognized educational commercial, industrial, and governmental institutions and organizations, and others legitimately engaged in educational pursuits, including training, testing, and measurement activities, may address a request for a licensing agreement to the copyright owners, who will determine whether, and under what conditions, including fees and charges, the materials in this book may be used by them. In other words, a licensing facility *exists* for the legitimate use of the material in this book on other than an individual basis. However, it is asseverated and affirmed here that the materials in this book *CANNOT* be used without the receipt of the express permission of such a licensing agreement from the Publishers.

NATIONAL LEARNING CORPORATION
212 Michael Drive
Syosset, New York 11791

Inquiries re licensing agreements should be addressed to:
  The President
  National Learning Corporation
  212 Michael Drive
  Syosset, New York 11791

PASSBOOK SERIES®

THE *PASSBOOK SERIES®* has been created to prepare applicants and candidates for the ultimate academic battlefield – the examination room.

At some time in our lives, each and every one of us may be required to take an examination – for validation, matriculation, admission, qualification, registration, certification, or licensure.

Based on the assumption that every applicant or candidate has met the basic formal educational standards, has taken the required number of courses, and read the necessary texts, the *PASSBOOK SERIES®* furnishes the one special preparation which may assure passing with confidence, instead of failing with insecurity. Examination questions – together with answers – are furnished as the basic vehicle for study so that the mysteries of the examination and its compounding difficulties may be eliminated or diminished by a sure method.

This book is meant to help you pass your examination provided that you qualify and are serious in your objective.

The entire field is reviewed through the huge store of content information which is succinctly presented through a provocative and challenging approach – the question-and-answer method.

A climate of success is established by furnishing the correct answers at the end of each test.

You soon learn to recognize types of questions, forms of questions, and patterns of questioning. You may even begin to anticipate expected outcomes.

You perceive that many questions are repeated or adapted so that you can gain acute insights, which may enable you to score many sure points.

You learn how to confront new questions, or types of questions, and to attack them confidently and work out the correct answers.

You note objectives and emphases, and recognize pitfalls and dangers, so that you may make positive educational adjustments.

Moreover, you are kept fully informed in relation to new concepts, methods, practices, and directions in the field.

You discover that you are actually taking the examination all the time: you are preparing for the examination by "taking" an examination, not by reading extraneous and/or supererogatory textbooks.

In short, this PASSBOOK®, used directedly, should be an important factor in helping you to pass your test.

PUBLIC INFORMATION OFFICER

<u>DUTIES</u>:
Prepares news stories and other informational material to be released to various
    news media including local newspapers, radio and television;
Edits writings and special promotional pieces and bulletins;
Contacts editors, radio program directors, publicity and advertising directors,
    civic organizations and others in furthering promotional and public
    relations activities of the county department or jurisdiction;
Prepares booklets, pamphlets, leaflets and other promotional literature as required;
Attends meetings of various related organizations to gather information on
    departmental or jurisdictional activities;
Prepares a variety of records and reports.

<u>SCOPE OF EXAMINATION</u>: Written test will cover knowledge, skills and/or abilities in
such areas as:

1. Directing a public information program or project;
2. Educating and interacting with the public;
3. Grammar, usage, punctuation and editing;
4. Format, layout and design of public information materials;
5. Preparing written material.

HOW TO TAKE A TEST

I. YOU MUST PASS AN EXAMINATION

A. *WHAT EVERY CANDIDATE SHOULD KNOW*

Examination applicants often ask us for help in preparing for the written test. What can I study in advance? What kinds of questions will be asked? How will the test be given? How will the papers be graded?

As an applicant for a civil service examination, you may be wondering about some of these things. Our purpose here is to suggest effective methods of advance study and to describe civil service examinations.

Your chances for success on this examination can be increased if you know how to prepare. Those "pre-examination jitters" can be reduced if you know what to expect. You can even experience an adventure in good citizenship if you know why civil service exams are given.

B. *WHY ARE CIVIL SERVICE EXAMINATIONS GIVEN?*

Civil service examinations are important to you in two ways. As a citizen, you want public jobs filled by employees who know how to do their work. As a job seeker, you want a fair chance to compete for that job on an equal footing with other candidates. The best-known means of accomplishing this two-fold goal is the competitive examination.

Exams are widely publicized throughout the nation. They may be administered for jobs in federal, state, city, municipal, town or village governments or agencies.

Any citizen may apply, with some limitations, such as the age or residence of applicants. Your experience and education may be reviewed to see whether you meet the requirements for the particular examination. When these requirements exist, they are reasonable and applied consistently to all applicants. Thus, a competitive examination may cause you some uneasiness now, but it is your privilege and safeguard.

C. *HOW ARE CIVIL SERVICE EXAMS DEVELOPED?*

Examinations are carefully written by trained technicians who are specialists in the field known as "psychological measurement," in consultation with recognized authorities in the field of work that the test will cover. These experts recommend the subject matter areas or skills to be tested; only those knowledges or skills important to your success on the job are included. The most reliable books and source materials available are used as references. Together, the experts and technicians judge the difficulty level of the questions.

Test technicians know how to phrase questions so that the problem is clearly stated. Their ethics do not permit "trick" or "catch" questions. Questions may have been tried out on sample groups, or subjected to statistical analysis, to determine their usefulness.

Written tests are often used in combination with performance tests, ratings of training and experience, and oral interviews. All of these measures combine to form the best-known means of finding the right person for the right job.

II. HOW TO PASS THE WRITTEN TEST

A. NATURE OF THE EXAMINATION

To prepare intelligently for civil service examinations, you should know how they differ from school examinations you have taken. In school you were assigned certain definite pages to read or subjects to cover. The examination questions were quite detailed and usually emphasized memory. Civil service exams, on the other hand, try to discover your present ability to perform the duties of a position, plus your potentiality to learn these duties. In other words, a civil service exam attempts to predict how successful you will be. Questions cover such a broad area that they cannot be as minute and detailed as school exam questions.

In the public service similar kinds of work, or positions, are grouped together in one "class." This process is known as *position-classification*. All the positions in a class are paid according to the salary range for that class. One class title covers all of these positions, and they are all tested by the same examination.

B. FOUR BASIC STEPS

1) Study the announcement

How, then, can you know what subjects to study? Our best answer is: "Learn as much as possible about the class of positions for which you've applied." The exam will test the knowledge, skills and abilities needed to do the work.

Your most valuable source of information about the position you want is the official exam announcement. This announcement lists the training and experience qualifications. Check these standards and apply only if you come reasonably close to meeting them.

The brief description of the position in the examination announcement offers some clues to the subjects which will be tested. Think about the job itself. Review the duties in your mind. Can you perform them, or are there some in which you are rusty? Fill in the blank spots in your preparation.

Many jurisdictions preview the written test in the exam announcement by including a section called "Knowledge and Abilities Required," "Scope of the Examination," or some similar heading. Here you will find out specifically what fields will be tested.

2) Review your own background

Once you learn in general what the position is all about, and what you need to know to do the work, ask yourself which subjects you already know fairly well and which need improvement. You may wonder whether to concentrate on improving your strong areas or on building some background in your fields of weakness. When the announcement has specified "some knowledge" or "considerable knowledge," or has used adjectives like "beginning principles of..." or "advanced ... methods," you can get a clue as to the number and difficulty of questions to be asked in any given field. More questions, and hence broader coverage, would be included for those subjects which are more important in the work. Now weigh your strengths and weaknesses against the job requirements and prepare accordingly.

3) Determine the level of the position

Another way to tell how intensively you should prepare is to understand the level of the job for which you are applying. Is it the entering level? In other words, is this the position in which beginners in a field of work are hired? Or is it an intermediate or advanced level? Sometimes this is indicated by such words as "Junior" or "Senior" in the class title. Other jurisdictions use Roman numerals to designate the level – Clerk I, Clerk II, for example. The word "Supervisor" sometimes appears in the title. If the level is not indicated by the title, check the description of duties. Will you be working under very close supervision, or will you have responsibility for independent decisions in this work?

4) Choose appropriate study materials

Now that you know the subjects to be examined and the relative amount of each subject to be covered, you can choose suitable study materials. For beginning level jobs, or even advanced ones, if you have a pronounced weakness in some aspect of your training, read a modern, standard textbook in that field. Be sure it is up to date and has general coverage. Such books are normally available at your library, and the librarian will be glad to help you locate one. For entry-level positions, questions of appropriate difficulty are chosen – neither highly advanced questions, nor those too simple. Such questions require careful thought but not advanced training.

If the position for which you are applying is technical or advanced, you will read more advanced, specialized material. If you are already familiar with the basic principles of your field, elementary textbooks would waste your time. Concentrate on advanced textbooks and technical periodicals. Think through the concepts and review difficult problems in your field.

These are all general sources. You can get more ideas on your own initiative, following these leads. For example, training manuals and publications of the government agency which employs workers in your field can be useful, particularly for technical and professional positions. A letter or visit to the government department involved may result in more specific study suggestions, and certainly will provide you with a more definite idea of the exact nature of the position you are seeking.

III. KINDS OF TESTS

Tests are used for purposes other than measuring knowledge and ability to perform specified duties. For some positions, it is equally important to test ability to make adjustments to new situations or to profit from training. In others, basic mental abilities not dependent on information are essential. Questions which test these things may not appear as pertinent to the duties of the position as those which test for knowledge and information. Yet they are often highly important parts of a fair examination. For very general questions, it is almost impossible to help you direct your study efforts. What we can do is to point out some of the more common of these general abilities needed in public service positions and describe some typical questions.

1) General information

Broad, general information has been found useful for predicting job success in some kinds of work. This is tested in a variety of ways, from vocabulary lists to questions about current events. Basic background in some field of work, such as sociology or economics, may be sampled in a group of questions. Often these are principles which have become familiar to most persons through exposure rather than through formal training. It is difficult to advise you how to study for these questions; being alert to the world around you is our best suggestion.

2) Verbal ability

An example of an ability needed in many positions is verbal or language ability. Verbal ability is, in brief, the ability to use and understand words. Vocabulary and grammar tests are typical measures of this ability. Reading comprehension or paragraph interpretation questions are common in many kinds of civil service tests. You are given a paragraph of written material and asked to find its central meaning.

3) Numerical ability

Number skills can be tested by the familiar arithmetic problem, by checking paired lists of numbers to see which are alike and which are different, or by interpreting charts and graphs. In the latter test, a graph may be printed in the test booklet which you are asked to use as the basis for answering questions.

4) Observation

A popular test for law-enforcement positions is the observation test. A picture is shown to you for several minutes, then taken away. Questions about the picture test your ability to observe both details and larger elements.

5) Following directions

In many positions in the public service, the employee must be able to carry out written instructions dependably and accurately. You may be given a chart with several columns, each column listing a variety of information. The questions require you to carry out directions involving the information given in the chart.

6) Skills and aptitudes

Performance tests effectively measure some manual skills and aptitudes. When the skill is one in which you are trained, such as typing or shorthand, you can practice. These tests are often very much like those given in business school or high school courses. For many of the other skills and aptitudes, however, no short-time preparation can be made. Skills and abilities natural to you or that you have developed throughout your lifetime are being tested.

Many of the general questions just described provide all the data needed to answer the questions and ask you to use your reasoning ability to find the answers. Your best preparation for these tests, as well as for tests of facts and ideas, is to be at your physical and mental best. You, no doubt, have your own methods of getting into an exam-taking mood and keeping "in shape." The next section lists some ideas on this subject.

IV. KINDS OF QUESTIONS

Only rarely is the "essay" question, which you answer in narrative form, used in civil service tests. Civil service tests are usually of the short-answer type. Full instructions for answering these questions will be given to you at the examination. But in case this is your first experience with short-answer questions and separate answer sheets, here is what you need to know:

1) Multiple-choice Questions

Most popular of the short-answer questions is the "multiple choice" or "best answer" question. It can be used, for example, to test for factual knowledge, ability to solve problems or judgment in meeting situations found at work.

A multiple-choice question is normally one of three types —

- It can begin with an incomplete statement followed by several possible endings. You are to find the one ending which *best* completes the statement, although some of the others may not be entirely wrong.
- It can also be a complete statement in the form of a question which is answered by choosing one of the statements listed.
- It can be in the form of a problem – again you select the best answer.

Here is an example of a multiple-choice question with a discussion which should give you some clues as to the method for choosing the right answer:

When an employee has a complaint about his assignment, the action which will *best* help him overcome his difficulty is to
   A. discuss his difficulty with his coworkers
   B. take the problem to the head of the organization
   C. take the problem to the person who gave him the assignment
   D. say nothing to anyone about his complaint

In answering this question, you should study each of the choices to find which is best. Consider choice "A" – Certainly an employee may discuss his complaint with fellow employees, but no change or improvement can result, and the complaint remains unresolved. Choice "B" is a poor choice since the head of the organization probably does not know what assignment you have been given, and taking your problem to him is known as "going over the head" of the supervisor. The supervisor, or person who made the assignment, is the person who can clarify it or correct any injustice. Choice "C" is, therefore, correct. To say nothing, as in choice "D," is unwise. Supervisors have and interest in knowing the problems employees are facing, and the employee is seeking a solution to his problem.

2) True/False Questions

The "true/false" or "right/wrong" form of question is sometimes used. Here a complete statement is given. Your job is to decide whether the statement is right or wrong.

SAMPLE: A person-to-person long-distance telephone call costs less than a station-to-station call to the same city.

This statement is wrong, or false, since person-to-person calls are more expensive.

This is not a complete list of all possible question forms, although most of the others are variations of these common types. You will always get complete directions for answering questions. Be sure you understand *how* to mark your answers – ask questions until you do.

V. RECORDING YOUR ANSWERS

For an examination with very few applicants, you may be told to record your answers in the test booklet itself. Separate answer sheets are much more common. If this separate answer sheet is to be scored by machine – and this is often the case – it is highly important that you mark your answers correctly in order to get credit.

An electric scoring machine is often used in civil service offices because of the speed with which papers can be scored. Machine-scored answer sheets must be marked with a pencil, which will be given to you. This pencil has a high graphite content which responds to the electric scoring machine. As a matter of fact, stray dots may register as answers, so do not let your pencil rest on the answer sheet while you are pondering the correct answer. Also, if your pencil lead breaks or is otherwise defective, ask for another.

Since the answer sheet will be dropped in a slot in the scoring machine, be careful not to bend the corners or get the paper crumpled.

The answer sheet normally has five vertical columns of numbers, with 30 numbers to a column. These numbers correspond to the question numbers in your test booklet. After each number, going across the page are four or five pairs of dotted lines. These short dotted lines have small letters or numbers above them. The first two pairs may also have a "T" or "F" above the letters. This indicates that the first two pairs only are to be used if the questions are of the true-false type. If the questions are multiple choice, disregard the "T" and "F" and pay attention only to the small letters or numbers.

Answer your questions in the manner of the sample that follows:

    32. The largest city in the United States is
        A. Washington, D.C.
        B. New York City
        C. Chicago
        D. Detroit
        E. San Francisco

1) Choose the answer you think is best. (New York City is the largest, so "B" is correct.)
2) Find the row of dotted lines numbered the same as the question you are answering. (Find row number 32)
3) Find the pair of dotted lines corresponding to the answer. (Find the pair of lines under the mark "B.")
4) Make a solid black mark between the dotted lines.

VI. BEFORE THE TEST

Common sense will help you find procedures to follow to get ready for an examination. Too many of us, however, overlook these sensible measures. Indeed, nervousness and fatigue have been found to be the most serious reasons why applicants fail to do their best on civil service tests. Here is a list of reminders:

- Begin your preparation early – Don't wait until the last minute to go scurrying around for books and materials or to find out what the position is all about.
- Prepare continuously – An hour a night for a week is better than an all-night cram session. This has been definitely established. What is more, a night a

week for a month will return better dividends than crowding your study into a shorter period of time.

- Locate the place of the exam – You have been sent a notice telling you when and where to report for the examination. If the location is in a different town or otherwise unfamiliar to you, it would be well to inquire the best route and learn something about the building.
- Relax the night before the test – Allow your mind to rest. Do not study at all that night. Plan some mild recreation or diversion; then go to bed early and get a good night's sleep.
- Get up early enough to make a leisurely trip to the place for the test – This way unforeseen events, traffic snarls, unfamiliar buildings, etc. will not upset you.
- Dress comfortably – A written test is not a fashion show. You will be known by number and not by name, so wear something comfortable.
- Leave excess paraphernalia at home – Shopping bags and odd bundles will get in your way. You need bring only the items mentioned in the official notice you received; usually everything you need is provided. Do not bring reference books to the exam. They will only confuse those last minutes and be taken away from you when in the test room.
- Arrive somewhat ahead of time – If because of transportation schedules you must get there very early, bring a newspaper or magazine to take your mind off yourself while waiting.
- Locate the examination room – When you have found the proper room, you will be directed to the seat or part of the room where you will sit. Sometimes you are given a sheet of instructions to read while you are waiting. Do not fill out any forms until you are told to do so; just read them and be prepared.
- Relax and prepare to listen to the instructions
- If you have any physical problem that may keep you from doing your best, be sure to tell the test administrator. If you are sick or in poor health, you really cannot do your best on the exam. You can come back and take the test some other time.

VII. AT THE TEST

The day of the test is here and you have the test booklet in your hand. The temptation to get going is very strong. Caution! There is more to success than knowing the right answers. You must know how to identify your papers and understand variations in the type of short-answer question used in this particular examination. Follow these suggestions for maximum results from your efforts:

1) Cooperate with the monitor
The test administrator has a duty to create a situation in which you can be as much at ease as possible. He will give instructions, tell you when to begin, check to see that you are marking your answer sheet correctly, and so on. He is not there to guard you, although he will see that your competitors do not take unfair advantage. He wants to help you do your best.

2) Listen to all instructions
Don't jump the gun! Wait until you understand all directions. In most civil service tests you get more time than you need to answer the questions. So don't be in a hurry.

Read each word of instructions until you clearly understand the meaning. Study the examples, listen to all announcements and follow directions. Ask questions if you do not understand what to do.

3) Identify your papers

Civil service exams are usually identified by number only. You will be assigned a number; you must not put your name on your test papers. Be sure to copy your number correctly. Since more than one exam may be given, copy your exact examination title.

4) Plan your time

Unless you are told that a test is a "speed" or "rate of work" test, speed itself is usually not important. Time enough to answer all the questions will be provided, but this does not mean that you have all day. An overall time limit has been set. Divide the total time (in minutes) by the number of questions to determine the approximate time you have for each question.

5) Do not linger over difficult questions

If you come across a difficult question, mark it with a paper clip (useful to have along) and come back to it when you have been through the booklet. One caution if you do this – be sure to skip a number on your answer sheet as well. Check often to be sure that you have not lost your place and that you are marking in the row numbered the same as the question you are answering.

6) Read the questions

Be sure you know what the question asks! Many capable people are unsuccessful because they failed to *read* the questions correctly.

7) Answer all questions

Unless you have been instructed that a penalty will be deducted for incorrect answers, it is better to guess than to omit a question.

8) Speed tests

It is often better NOT to guess on speed tests. It has been found that on timed tests people are tempted to spend the last few seconds before time is called in marking answers at random – without even reading them – in the hope of picking up a few extra points. To discourage this practice, the instructions may warn you that your score will be "corrected" for guessing. That is, a penalty will be applied. The incorrect answers will be deducted from the correct ones, or some other penalty formula will be used.

9) Review your answers

If you finish before time is called, go back to the questions you guessed or omitted to give them further thought. Review other answers if you have time.

10) Return your test materials

If you are ready to leave before others have finished or time is called, take ALL your materials to the monitor and leave quietly. Never take any test material with you. The monitor can discover whose papers are not complete, and taking a test booklet may be grounds for disqualification.

VIII. EXAMINATION TECHNIQUES

1) Read the general instructions carefully. These are usually printed on the first page of the exam booklet. As a rule, these instructions refer to the timing of the examination; the fact that you should not start work until the signal and must stop work at a signal, etc. If there are any *special* instructions, such as a choice of questions to be answered, make sure that you note this instruction carefully.

2) When you are ready to start work on the examination, that is as soon as the signal has been given, read the instructions to each question booklet, underline any key words or phrases, such as *least*, *best*, *outline*, *describe* and the like. In this way you will tend to answer as requested rather than discover on reviewing your paper that you *listed without describing*, that you selected the *worst* choice rather than the *best* choice, etc.

3) If the examination is of the objective or multiple-choice type – that is, each question will also give a series of possible answers: A, B, C or D, and you are called upon to select the best answer and write the letter next to that answer on your answer paper – it is advisable to start answering each question in turn. There may be anywhere from 50 to 100 such questions in the three or four hours allotted and you can see how much time would be taken if you read through all the questions before beginning to answer any. Furthermore, if you come across a question or group of questions which you know would be difficult to answer, it would undoubtedly affect your handling of all the other questions.

4) If the examination is of the essay type and contains but a few questions, it is a moot point as to whether you should read all the questions before starting to answer any one. Of course, if you are given a choice – say five out of seven and the like – then it is essential to read all the questions so you can eliminate the two that are most difficult. If, however, you are asked to answer all the questions, there may be danger in trying to answer the easiest one first because you may find that you will spend too much time on it. The best technique is to answer the first question, then proceed to the second, etc.

5) Time your answers. Before the exam begins, write down the time it started, then add the time allowed for the examination and write down the time it must be completed, then divide the time available somewhat as follows:
   - If 3-1/2 hours are allowed, that would be 210 minutes. If you have 80 objective-type questions, that would be an average of 2-1/2 minutes per question. Allow yourself no more than 2 minutes per question, or a total of 160 minutes, which will permit about 50 minutes to review.
   - If for the time allotment of 210 minutes there are 7 essay questions to answer, that would average about 30 minutes a question. Give yourself only 25 minutes per question so that you have about 35 minutes to review.

6) The most important instruction is to *read each question* and make sure you know what is wanted. The second most important instruction is to *time yourself properly* so that you answer every question. The third most

important instruction is to *answer every question.* Guess if you have to but include something for each question. Remember that you will receive no credit for a blank and will probably receive some credit if you write something in answer to an essay question. If you guess a letter – say "B" for a multiple-choice question – you may have guessed right. If you leave a blank as an answer to a multiple-choice question, the examiners may respect your feelings but it will not add a point to your score. Some exams may penalize you for wrong answers, so in such cases *only*, you may not want to guess unless you have some basis for your answer.

7) Suggestions
  a. Objective-type questions
    1. Examine the question booklet for proper sequence of pages and questions
    2. Read all instructions carefully
    3. Skip any question which seems too difficult; return to it after all other questions have been answered
    4. Apportion your time properly; do not spend too much time on any single question or group of questions
    5. Note and underline key words – *all, most, fewest, least, best, worst, same, opposite,* etc.
    6. Pay particular attention to negatives
    7. Note unusual option, e.g., unduly long, short, complex, different or similar in content to the body of the question
    8. Observe the use of "hedging" words – *probably, may, most likely,* etc.
    9. Make sure that your answer is put next to the same number as the question
    10. Do not second-guess unless you have good reason to believe the second answer is definitely more correct
    11. Cross out original answer if you decide another answer is more accurate; do not erase until you are ready to hand your paper in
    12. Answer all questions; guess unless instructed otherwise
    13. Leave time for review

  b. Essay questions
    1. Read each question carefully
    2. Determine exactly what is wanted. Underline key words or phrases.
    3. Decide on outline or paragraph answer
    4. Include many different points and elements unless asked to develop any one or two points or elements
    5. Show impartiality by giving pros and cons unless directed to select one side only
    6. Make and write down any assumptions you find necessary to answer the questions
    7. Watch your English, grammar, punctuation and choice of words
    8. Time your answers; don't crowd material

8) Answering the essay question

Most essay questions can be answered by framing the specific response around several key words or ideas. Here are a few such key words or ideas:

M's: manpower, materials, methods, money, management

P's: purpose, program, policy, plan, procedure, practice, problems, pitfalls, personnel, public relations

    a. Six basic steps in handling problems:
1. Preliminary plan and background development
2. Collect information, data and facts
3. Analyze and interpret information, data and facts
4. Analyze and develop solutions as well as make recommendations
5. Prepare report and sell recommendations
6. Install recommendations and follow up effectiveness

    b. Pitfalls to avoid
1. *Taking things for granted* – A statement of the situation does not necessarily imply that each of the elements is necessarily true; for example, a complaint may be invalid and biased so that all that can be taken for granted is that a complaint has been registered
2. *Considering only one side of a situation* – Wherever possible, indicate several alternatives and then point out the reasons you selected the best one
3. *Failing to indicate follow up* – Whenever your answer indicates action on your part, make certain that you will take proper follow-up action to see how successful your recommendations, procedures or actions turn out to be
4. *Taking too long in answering any single question* – Remember to time your answers properly

IX. AFTER THE TEST

Scoring procedures differ in detail among civil service jurisdictions although the general principles are the same. Whether the papers are hand-scored or graded by machine we have described, they are nearly always graded by number. That is, the person who marks the paper knows only the number – never the name – of the applicant. Not until all the papers have been graded will they be matched with names. If other tests, such as training and experience or oral interview ratings have been given, scores will be combined. Different parts of the examination usually have different weights. For example, the written test might count 60 percent of the final grade, and a rating of training and experience 40 percent. In many jurisdictions, veterans will have a certain number of points added to their grades.

After the final grade has been determined, the names are placed in grade order and an eligible list is established. There are various methods for resolving ties between those who get the same final grade – probably the most common is to place first the name of the person whose application was received first. Job offers are made from the eligible list in the order the names appear on it. You will be notified of your grade and your rank as soon as all these computations have been made. This will be done as rapidly as possible.

People who are found to meet the requirements in the announcement are called "eligibles." Their names are put on a list of eligible candidates. An eligible's chances of getting a job depend on how high he stands on this list and how fast agencies are filling jobs from the list.

When a job is to be filled from a list of eligibles, the agency asks for the names of people on the list of eligibles for that job. When the civil service commission receives this request, it sends to the agency the names of the three people highest on this list. Or, if the job to be filled has specialized requirements, the office sends the agency the names of the top three persons who meet these requirements from the general list.

The appointing officer makes a choice from among the three people whose names were sent to him. If the selected person accepts the appointment, the names of the others are put back on the list to be considered for future openings.

That is the rule in hiring from all kinds of eligible lists, whether they are for typist, carpenter, chemist, or something else. For every vacancy, the appointing officer has his choice of any one of the top three eligibles on the list. This explains why the person whose name is on top of the list sometimes does not get an appointment when some of the persons lower on the list do. If the appointing officer chooses the second or third eligible, the No. 1 eligible does not get a job at once, but stays on the list until he is appointed or the list is terminated.

X. HOW TO PASS THE INTERVIEW TEST

The examination for which you applied requires an oral interview test. You have already taken the written test and you are now being called for the interview test – the final part of the formal examination.

You may think that it is not possible to prepare for an interview test and that there are no procedures to follow during an interview. Our purpose is to point out some things you can do in advance that will help you and some good rules to follow and pitfalls to avoid while you are being interviewed.

What is an interview supposed to test?

The written examination is designed to test the technical knowledge and competence of the candidate; the oral is designed to evaluate intangible qualities, not readily measured otherwise, and to establish a list showing the relative fitness of each candidate – as measured against his competitors – for the position sought. Scoring is not on the basis of "right" and "wrong," but on a sliding scale of values ranging from "not passable" to "outstanding." As a matter of fact, it is possible to achieve a relatively low score without a single "incorrect" answer because of evident weakness in the qualities being measured.

Occasionally, an examination may consist entirely of an oral test – either an individual or a group oral. In such cases, information is sought concerning the technical knowledges and abilities of the candidate, since there has been no written examination for this purpose. More commonly, however, an oral test is used to supplement a written examination.

Who conducts interviews?

The composition of oral boards varies among different jurisdictions. In nearly all, a representative of the personnel department serves as chairman. One of the members of the board may be a representative of the department in which the candidate would work. In some cases, "outside experts" are used, and, frequently, a businessman or some other representative of the general public is asked to serve. Labor and management or other special groups may be represented. The aim is to secure the services of experts in the appropriate field.

However the board is composed, it is a good idea (and not at all improper or unethical) to ascertain in advance of the interview who the members are and what groups they represent. When you are introduced to them, you will have some idea of their backgrounds and interests, and at least you will not stutter and stammer over their names.

What should be done before the interview?

While knowledge about the board members is useful and takes some of the surprise element out of the interview, there is other preparation which is more substantive. It *is* possible to prepare for an oral interview – in several ways:

1) Keep a copy of your application and review it carefully before the interview

This may be the only document before the oral board, and the starting point of the interview. Know what education and experience you have listed there, and the sequence and dates of all of it. Sometimes the board will ask you to review the highlights of your experience for them; you should not have to hem and haw doing it.

2) Study the class specification and the examination announcement

Usually, the oral board has one or both of these to guide them. The qualities, characteristics or knowledges required by the position sought are stated in these documents. They offer valuable clues as to the nature of the oral interview. For example, if the job involves supervisory responsibilities, the announcement will usually indicate that knowledge of modern supervisory methods and the qualifications of the candidate as a supervisor will be tested. If so, you can expect such questions, frequently in the form of a hypothetical situation which you are expected to solve. NEVER go into an oral without knowledge of the duties and responsibilities of the job you seek.

3) Think through each qualification required

Try to visualize the kind of questions you would ask if you were a board member. How well could you answer them? Try especially to appraise your own knowledge and background in each area, *measured against the job sought*, and identify any areas in which you are weak. Be critical and realistic – do not flatter yourself.

4) Do some general reading in areas in which you feel you may be weak

For example, if the job involves supervision and your past experience has NOT, some general reading in supervisory methods and practices, particularly in the field of human relations, might be useful. Do NOT study agency procedures or detailed manuals. The oral board will be testing your understanding and capacity, not your memory.

5) Get a good night's sleep and watch your general health and mental attitude

You will want a clear head at the interview. Take care of a cold or any other minor ailment, and of course, no hangovers.

What should be done on the day of the interview?

Now comes the day of the interview itself. Give yourself plenty of time to get there. Plan to arrive somewhat ahead of the scheduled time, particularly if your appointment is in the fore part of the day. If a previous candidate fails to appear, the board might be ready for you a bit early. By early afternoon an oral board is almost invariably behind schedule if there are many candidates, and you may have to wait.

Take along a book or magazine to read, or your application to review, but leave any extraneous material in the waiting room when you go in for your interview. In any event, relax and compose yourself.

The matter of dress is important. The board is forming impressions about you – from your experience, your manners, your attitude, and your appearance. Give your personal appearance careful attention. Dress your best, but not your flashiest. Choose conservative, appropriate clothing, and be sure it is immaculate. This is a business interview, and your appearance should indicate that you regard it as such. Besides, being well groomed and properly dressed will help boost your confidence.

Sooner or later, someone will call your name and escort you into the interview room. *This is it.* From here on you are on your own. It is too late for any more preparation. But remember, you asked for this opportunity to prove your fitness, and you are here because your request was granted.

What happens when you go in?

The usual sequence of events will be as follows: The clerk (who is often the board stenographer) will introduce you to the chairman of the oral board, who will introduce you to the other members of the board. Acknowledge the introductions before you sit down. Do not be surprised if you find a microphone facing you or a stenotypist sitting by. Oral interviews are usually recorded in the event of an appeal or other review.

Usually the chairman of the board will open the interview by reviewing the highlights of your education and work experience from your application – primarily for the benefit of the other members of the board, as well as to get the material into the record. Do not interrupt or comment unless there is an error or significant misinterpretation; if that is the case, do not hesitate. But do not quibble about insignificant matters. Also, he will usually ask you some question about your education, experience or your present job – partly to get you to start talking and to establish the interviewing "rapport." He may start the actual questioning, or turn it over to one of the other members. Frequently, each member undertakes the questioning on a particular area, one in which he is perhaps most competent, so you can expect each member to participate in the examination. Because time is limited, you may also expect some rather abrupt switches in the direction the questioning takes, so do not be upset by it. Normally, a board member will not pursue a single line of questioning unless he discovers a particular strength or weakness.

After each member has participated, the chairman will usually ask whether any member has any further questions, then will ask you if you have anything you wish to add. Unless you are expecting this question, it may floor you. Worse, it may start you off on an extended, extemporaneous speech. The board is not usually seeking more information. The question is principally to offer you a last opportunity to present further qualifications or to indicate that you have nothing to add. So, if you feel that a significant qualification or characteristic has been overlooked, it is proper to point it out in a sentence or so. Do not compliment the board on the thoroughness of their examination – they have been sketchy, and you know it. If you wish, merely say, "No thank you, I have nothing further to add." This is a point where you can "talk yourself out" of a good impression or fail to present an important bit of information. Remember, *you close the interview yourself.*

The chairman will then say, "That is all, Mr. _____, thank you." Do not be startled; the interview is over, and quicker than you think. Thank him, gather your belongings and take your leave. Save your sigh of relief for the other side of the door.

How to put your best foot forward

Throughout this entire process, you may feel that the board individually and collectively is trying to pierce your defenses, seek out your hidden weaknesses and embarrass and confuse you. Actually, this is not true. They are obliged to make an appraisal of your qualifications for the job you are seeking, and they want to see you in your best light. Remember, they must interview all candidates and a non-cooperative candidate may become a failure in spite of their best efforts to bring out his qualifications. Here are 15 suggestions that will help you:

1) Be natural – Keep your attitude confident, not cocky

If you are not confident that you can do the job, do not expect the board to be. Do not apologize for your weaknesses, try to bring out your strong points. The board is interested in a positive, not negative, presentation. Cockiness will antagonize any board member and make him wonder if you are covering up a weakness by a false show of strength.

2) Get comfortable, but don't lounge or sprawl

Sit erectly but not stiffly. A careless posture may lead the board to conclude that you are careless in other things, or at least that you are not impressed by the importance of the occasion. Either conclusion is natural, even if incorrect. Do not fuss with your clothing, a pencil or an ashtray. Your hands may occasionally be useful to emphasize a point; do not let them become a point of distraction.

3) Do not wisecrack or make small talk

This is a serious situation, and your attitude should show that you consider it as such. Further, the time of the board is limited – they do not want to waste it, and neither should you.

4) Do not exaggerate your experience or abilities

In the first place, from information in the application or other interviews and sources, the board may know more about you than you think. Secondly, you probably will not get away with it. An experienced board is rather adept at spotting such a situation, so do not take the chance.

5) If you know a board member, do not make a point of it, yet do not hide it

Certainly you are not fooling him, and probably not the other members of the board. Do not try to take advantage of your acquaintanceship – it will probably do you little good.

6) Do not dominate the interview

Let the board do that. They will give you the clues – do not assume that you have to do all the talking. Realize that the board has a number of questions to ask you, and do not try to take up all the interview time by showing off your extensive knowledge of the answer to the first one.

7) Be attentive

You only have 20 minutes or so, and you should keep your attention at its sharpest throughout. When a member is addressing a problem or question to you, give him your undivided attention. Address your reply principally to him, but do not exclude the other board members.

8) Do not interrupt

A board member may be stating a problem for you to analyze. He will ask you a question when the time comes. Let him state the problem, and wait for the question.

9) Make sure you understand the question

Do not try to answer until you are sure what the question is. If it is not clear, restate it in your own words or ask the board member to clarify it for you. However, do not haggle about minor elements.

10) Reply promptly but not hastily

A common entry on oral board rating sheets is "candidate responded readily," or "candidate hesitated in replies." Respond as promptly and quickly as you can, but do not jump to a hasty, ill-considered answer.

11) Do not be peremptory in your answers

A brief answer is proper – but do not fire your answer back. That is a losing game from your point of view. The board member can probably ask questions much faster than you can answer them.

12) Do not try to create the answer you think the board member wants

He is interested in what kind of mind you have and how it works – not in playing games. Furthermore, he can usually spot this practice and will actually grade you down on it.

13) Do not switch sides in your reply merely to agree with a board member

Frequently, a member will take a contrary position merely to draw you out and to see if you are willing and able to defend your point of view. Do not start a debate, yet do not surrender a good position. If a position is worth taking, it is worth defending.

14) Do not be afraid to admit an error in judgment if you are shown to be wrong

The board knows that you are forced to reply without any opportunity for careful consideration. Your answer may be demonstrably wrong. If so, admit it and get on with the interview.

15) Do not dwell at length on your present job

The opening question may relate to your present assignment. Answer the question but do not go into an extended discussion. You are being examined for a *new* job, not your present one. As a matter of fact, try to phrase ALL your answers in terms of the job for which you are being examined.

Basis of Rating

Probably you will forget most of these "do's" and "don'ts" when you walk into the oral interview room. Even remembering them all will not ensure you a passing grade. Perhaps you did not have the qualifications in the first place. But remembering them will help you to put your best foot forward, without treading on the toes of the board members.

Rumor and popular opinion to the contrary notwithstanding, an oral board wants you to make the best appearance possible. They know you are under pressure – but they also want to see how you respond to it as a guide to what your reaction would be under the pressures of the job you seek. They will be influenced by the degree of poise you display, the personal traits you show and the manner in which you respond.

EXAMINATION SECTION

EXAMINATION SECTION
TEST 1

Directions: Each question or incomplete statement is followed by several suggested answers or completions. Select the one that BEST answers the question or completes the statement. *PRINT THE LETTER OF THE CORRECT ANSWER IN THE SPACE AT THE RIGHT.*

1)   When conducting a needs assessment for the purpose of education planning, an agency's FIRST step is to identify or provide

1. _____

A.   a profile of population characteristics
B.   barriers to participation
C.   existing resources
D.   profiles of competing resources

2)   Research has demonstrated that of the following, the most effective medium for communicating with external publics is/are

2. _____

A.   video news releases
B.   television
C.   radio
D.   newspapers

3)   Basic ideas behind the effort to influence the attitudes and behaviors of a constituency include each of the following, EXCEPT the idea that

3. _____

A.   words, rather than actions or events, are most likely to motivate
B.   demands for action are a usual response
C.   self-interest usually figures heavily into public involvement
D.   the reliability of change programs is difficult to assess

4)   An agency representative is trying to craft a pithy message to constituents in order to encourage the use agency program resources. Choosing an audience for such messages is easiest when the message

4. _____

A.   is project- or behavior-based
B.   is combined with other messages
C.   is abstract
D.   has a broad appeal

5)   Of the following factors, the most important to the success of an   5. _____
agency's external education or communication programs is the

A.   amount of resources used to implement them
B.   public's prior experiences with the agency
C.   real value of the program to the public
D.   commitment of the internal audience

6)   A representative for a state agency is being interviewed by a reporter   6. _____
from a local news network. The representative is being asked to defend a program that is extremely unpopular in certain parts of the municipality. When a
constituency is known to be opposed to a position, the most useful communication strategy is to present

A.   only the arguments that are consistent with constituents' views
B.   only the agency's side of the issue
C.   both sides of the argument as clearly as possible
D.   both sides of the argument, omitting key information about the oppos-
ing position

7)   The most significant barriers to effective agency community relations   7. _____
include

        I.   widespread distrust of communication strategies
        II.   the media's "watchdog" stance
        III.   public apathy
        IV.   statutory opposition

A.   I only
B.   I and II
C.   II and III
D.   III and IV

8)   In conducting an education program, many agencies use workshops   8. _____
and seminars in a classroom setting. Advantages of classroom-style teach-
ing over other means of educating the public include each of the following,
EXCEPT:

A.   enabling an instructor to verify learning through testing and interaction
with the target audience
B.   enabling hands-on practice and other participatory learning techniques
C.   ability to reach an unlimited number of participants in a given length
of time
D.   ability to convey the latest, most up-to-date information

9) The _____ model of community relations is character-   9. _____
ized by an attempt to persuade the public to adopt the agency's point of view.

A.   two-way symmetric
B.   two-way asymmetric
C.   public information
D.   press agency/publicity

10)   Important elements of an internal situation analysis include the   10. _____

    I.   list of agency opponents
    II.   communication audit
    III.   updated organizational almanac
    IV.   stakeholder analysis

A.   I and II
B.   I, II and III
C.   II and III
D.   I, II, III and IV

11)   Government agency information efforts typically involve each of the   11. _____
following objectives, EXCEPT to

A.   implement changes in the policies of government agencies to align
with public opinion
B.   communicate the work of agencies
C.   explain agency techniques in a way that invites input from citizens
D.   provide citizen feedback to government administrators

12)   Factors that are likely to influence the effectiveness of an educational   12. _____
campaign include the

    I.   level of homogeneity among intended participants
    II.   number and types of media used
    III.   receptivity of the intended participants
    IV.   level of specificity in the message or behavior to be taught

A.   I and II
B.   I, II and III
C.   II and III
D.   I, II, III and IV

13) An agency representative is writing instructional objectives that will   13. _____
later help to measure the effectiveness of an educational program. Which of
the following verbs, included in an objective, would be MOST helpful for the
purpose of measuring effectiveness?

A.   Know
B.   Identify
C.   Learn
D.   Comprehend

14) A state education agency wants to encourage participation in a pro-   14. _____
gram that has just received a boost through new federal legislation. The program is intended to include participants from a wide variety of socioeconomic
and other demographic characteristics.

    The agency wants to launch a broad-based program that will inform
virtually every interested party in the state about the program's new circumstances. In attempting to deliver this message to such a wide-ranging constituency, the agency's best practice would be to

A.   broadcast the same message through as many different media channels
as possible
B.   focus on one discrete segment of the public at a time
C.   craft a message whose appeal is as broad as the public itself
D.   let the program's achievements speak for themselves and rely on word-
of-mouth

15) Advantages associated with using the World Wide Web as an educa-   15. _____
tional tool include

    I.   an appeal to younger generations of the public
    II.   visually-oriented, interactive learning
    III.   learning that is not confined by space, time, or institutional as
          sociation
    IV.   a variety of methods for verifying use and learning

A.   I only
B.   I and II
C.   I, II and III
D.   I, II, III and IV

16)   In agencies involved in health care, community relations is a critical   16. _____
function because it

A.   serves as an intermediary between the agency and consumers
B.   generates a clear mission statement for agency goals and priorities
C.   ensures patient privacy while satisfying the media's right to informa-
tion
D.   helps marketing professionals determine the wants and needs of
agency constituents

17)   After an extensive campaign to promote its newest program to con-   17. _____
stituents, an agency learns that most of the audience did not understand the
intended message. Most likely, the agency has

A.   chosen words that were intended to inform, rather than persuade
B.   not accurately interpreted what the audience really needed to know
C.   overestimated the ability of the audience to receive and process the
message
D.   compensated for noise that may have interrupted the message

18)   The necessary elements that lead to conviction and motivation in the   18. _____
minds of participants in an educational or information program include each
of the following, EXCEPT the _____ of the message.

A.   acceptability
B.   intensity
C.   single-channel appeal
D.   pervasiveness

19)   Printed materials are often at the core of educational programs provid-   19. _____
ed by public agencies. The primary disadvantage associated with print is that
it

A.   does not enable comprehensive treatment of a topic
B.   is generally unreliable in term of assessing results
C.   is often the most expensive medium available
D.   is constrained by time

20)   Traditional thinking on public opinion holds that there is about ___   20. _____
_____ percent of the public who are pivotal to shifting the balance and mo-
mentum of opinion—they are concerned about an issue, but not fanatical, and
interested enough to pay attention to a reasoned discussion.

A.   2
B.   10
C.   33
D.   51

21) One of the most useful guidelines for influencing attitude change among people is to

21. _____

A. inviting the target audience to come to you, rather than approaching them
B. use moral appeals as the primary approach
C. use concrete images to enable people to see the results of behaviors or indifference
D. offer tangible rewards to people for changes in behaviors

22) An agency is attempting to evaluate the effectiveness of its educational program. For this purpose, it wants to observe several focus groups discussing the same program. Which of the following would NOT be a guideline for the use of focus groups?

22. _____

A. Focus groups should only include those who have participated in the program.
B. Be sure to accurately record the discussion.
C. The same questions should be asked at each focus group meeting.
D. It is often helpful to have a neutral, non-agency employee facilitate discussions.

23) Research consistently shows that _____ is the determinant most likely to make a newspaper editor run a news release.

23. _____

A. novelty
B. prominence
C. proximity
D. conflict

24) Which of the following is NOT one of the major variables to take into account when considering a population needs assessment?

24. _____

A. State of program development
B. Resources available
C. Demographics
D. Community attitudes

25) The first step in any communications audit is to

25. _____

A. develop a research instrument
B. determine how the organization currently communicates
C. hire a contractor
D. determine which audience to assess

KEY (CORRECT ANSWERS)

1. A
2. D
3. A
4. A
5. D

6. C
7. D
8. C
9. B
10. C

11. A
12. D
13. B
14. B
15. C

16. A
17. B
18. C
19. B
20. B

21. C
22. A
23. C
24. C
25. D

TEST 2

Directions: Each question or incomplete statement is followed by several suggested answers or completions. Select the one that BEST answers the question or completes the statement. *PRINT THE LETTER OF THE CORRECT ANSWER IN THE SPACE AT THE RIGHT.*

1) A public relations practitioner at an agency has just composed a press release highlighting a program's recent accomplishments and success stories. In pitching such releases to print outlets, the practitioner should

    I.   e-mail, mail, or send them by messenger
    II.   address them to "editor" or "news director"
    III.   have an assistant call all media contacts by telephone
    IV.   ask reporters or editors how they prefer to receive them

A. I and II
B. I and IV
C. II, III and IV
D. III only

1. _____

2) The "output goals" of an educational program are MOST likely to include

A. specified ratings of services by participants on a standardized scale
B. observable effects on a given community or clientele
C. the number of instructional hours provided
D. the number of participants served

2. _____

3) An agency wants to evaluate satisfaction levels among program participants, and mails out questionnaires to everyone who has been enrolled in the last year. The primary problem associated with this method of evaluative research is that it

A. poses a significant inconvenience for respondents
B. is inordinately expensive
C. does not allow for follow-up or clarification questions
D. usually involves a low response rate

3. _____

4) A communications audit is an important tool for measuring

A. the depth of penetration of a particular message or program
B. the cost of the organization's information campaigns
C. how key audiences perceive an organization
D. the commitment of internal stakeholders

4. _____

5) The "ABC's" of written learning objectives include each of the following, EXCEPT

5. _____

A. Audience
B. Behavior
C. Conditions
D. Delineation

6) When attempting to change the behaviors of constituents, it is important to keep in mind that

6. _____

    I. most people are skeptical of communications that try to get them to change their behaviors
    II. in most cases, a person selects the media to which he exposes himself
    III. people tend to react defensively to messages or programs that rely on fear as a motivating factor
    IV. programs should aim for the broadest appeal possible in order to include as many participants as possible

A. I and II
B. I, II and III
C. II and III
D. I, II, III and IV

7) The "laws" of public opinion include the idea that it is

7. _____

A. useful for anticipating emergencies
B. not sensitive to important events
C. basically determined by self-interest
D. sustainable through persistent appeals

8) Which of the following types of evaluations is used to measure public attitudes before and after an information/educational program?

8. _____

A. retrieval study
B. copy test
C. quota sampling
D. benchmark study

9) The primary source for internal communications is/are usually

9. _____

A. flow charts
B. meetings
C. voice mail
D. printed publications

10)   An agency representative is putting together informational materials—   10. _____
brochures and a newsletter—outlining changes in one of the state's biggest
benefits programs. In assembling print materials as a medium for delivering
information to the public, the representative should keep in mind each of the
following trends:

      I.   For various reasons, the reading capabilities of the public are in
             general decline
      II.   Without tables and graphs to help illustrate the changes, it is
             unlikely that the message will be delivered effectively
      III.   Professionals and career-oriented people are highly receptive to
             information written in the form of a journal article or empirical
             study
      IV.   People tend to be put off by print materials that use itemized
             and bulleted (•) lists.

A.   I and II
B.   I, II and III
C.   II and III
D.   I, II, III and IV

11)   Which of the following steps in a problem-oriented information cam-   11. _____
paign would typically be implemented FIRST?

A.   Deciding on tactics
B.   Determining a communications strategy
C.   Evaluating the problem's impact
D.   Developing an organizational strategy

12)   A common pitfall in conducting an educational program is to   12. _____

A.   aim it at the wrong target audience
B.   overfund it
C.   leave it in the hands of people who are in the business of education,
rather than those with expertise in the business of the organization
D.   ignore the possibility that some other organization is meeting the same
educational need for the target audience

13)   The key factors that affect the credibility of an agency's educational   13. _____
program include

A.   organization
B.   scope
C.   sophistication
D.   penetration

14)   Research on public opinion consistently demonstrates that it is   14. _____

A.   easy to move people toward a strong opinion on anything, as long as
they are approached directly through their emotions
B.   easier to move people away from an opinion they currently hold than
to have them form an opinion about something they have not previously cared
about
C.   easy to move people toward a strong opinion on anything, as long as
the message appeals to their reason and intellect
D.   difficult to move people toward a strong opinion on anything, no matter what the approach

15)   In conducting an education program, many agencies use meetings and   15. _____
conferences to educate an audience about the organization and its programs.
Advantages associated with this approach include

        I.   a captive audience that is known to be interested in the topic
        II.   ample opportunities for verifying learning
        III.   cost-efficient meeting space
        IV.   the ability to provide information on a wider variety of subjects

A.   I and II
B.   I, III and IV
C.   II and III
D.   I, II, III and IV

16)   An agency is attempting to evaluate the effectiveness of its educational   16. _____
programs. For this purpose, it wants to observe several focus groups discussing particular programs. For this purpose, a focus group should never number
more than _____ participants.

A.   5
B.   10
C.   15
D.   20

17)   A _____ speech is written so that several agency members   17. _____
can deliver it to different audiences with only minor variations.

A.   basic
B.   printed
C.   quota
D.   pattern

18)	Which of the following statements about public opinion is generally	18. _____
considered to be FALSE?

A.	Opinion is primarily reactive rather than proactive.
B.	People have more opinions about goals than about the means by which
to achieve them.
C.	Facts tend to shift opinion in the accepted direction when opinion is
not solidly structured.
D.	Public opinion is based more on information than desire.

19)	An agency is trying to promote its educational program. As a general	19. _____
rule, the agency should NOT assume that

A.	people will only participate if they perceive an individual benefit
B.	promotions need to be aimed at small, discrete groups
C.	if the program is good, the audience will find out about it
D.	a variety of methods, including advertising, special events, and direct
mail, should be considered

20)	In planning a successful educational program, probably the first and	20. _____
most important question for an agency to ask is:

A.	What will be the content of the program?
B.	Who will be served by the program?
C.	When is the best time to schedule the program?
D.	Why is the program necessary?

21)	Media kits are LEAST likely to contain	21. _____

A.	fact sheets
B.	memoranda
C.	photographs with captions
D.	news releases

22)	The use of pamphlets and booklets as media for communication with	22. _____
the public often involves the disadvantage that

A.	the messages contained within them are frequently nonspecific
B.	it is difficult to measure their effectiveness in delivering the message
C.	there are few opportunities for people to refer to them
D.	color reproduction is poor

23) The most important prerequisite of a good educational program is an   23. _____

A.   abundance of resources to implement it
B.   individual staff unit formed for the purpose of program delivery
C.   accurate needs assessment
D.   uneducated constituency

24) After an education program has been delivered, an agency conducts a   24. _____
program evaluation to determine whether its objectives have been met. General rules about how to conduct such an education program evaluation include each of the following, EXCEPT that it

A.   must be done immediately after the program has been implemented
B.   should be simple and easy to use
C.   should be designed so that tabulation of responses can take place
quickly and inexpensively
D.   should solicit mostly subjective, open-ended responses if the audience
was large

25) Using electronic media such as television as means of educating the   25. _____
public is typically recommended ONLY for agencies that

I.   have a fairly simple message to begin with
II.   want to reach the masses, rather than a targeted audience
III. have substantial financial resources
IV.   accept that they will not be able to measure the results of the
      campaign with much precision

A.   I and II
B.   I, II and III
C.   II and IV
D.   I, II, III and IV

KEY (CORRECT ANSWERS)

1. B
2. C
3. D
4. C
5. D

6. B
7. C
8. D
9. D
10. A

11. C
12. D
13. A
14. D
15. B

16. B
17. D
18. D
19. C
20. D

21. B
22. B
23. C
24. D
25. D

EXAMINATION SECTION

TEST 1

1. The informed editorial assistant knows that the difference between a copy reader and a proofreader is that the copy reader
   A. checks copy against type proofs
   B. checks galleys
   C. edits material submitted by writers
   D. holds copy for the proofreader

   1.___

2. *Style* to a copy editor means
   A. following a set pattern when rules of spelling and punctuation are equivocal
   B. following the rules of formal grammar
   C. making sure that the writing is not *elegant*
   D. making sure that the writing is polished

   2.___

3. Before it is sent to the composing room, each page of copy *MUST* be
   A. copy edited   B. galley proofed
   C. given a folio number D. proofread

   3.___

4. When a long paragraph in a manuscript is to be divided into two paragraphs, it should be done
   A. by circling the first word of the new paragraph
   B. by marking an ℙ around the beginning of the new paragraph
   C. by marking dividing spot with caret and writing note to printer in margin
   D. with paste pot and shears at point of division

   4.___

5. To a copy editor, the word *more* means
   A. facts are insufficient
   B. linotypists need copy to keep machines running
   C. story goes to next take
   D. story is not long enough

   5.___

6. To abbreviate the word *Company*, as in Jones Widget Company, a copy editor should
   A. circle the word
   B. cross out excess letters and put a period over the *m*
   C. cross out the entire word and write *Co.* above it in the space between the lines
   D. cross out the entire word and write *Co.* in margin, running a line to its position

   6.___

7. In editing copy, it is often necessary to indicate that   7.__
   numerals are to be spelled out.
   This is done by
      A. circling the numeral
      B. crossing out the numeral and spelling it out between the
         lines
      C. crossing out the numeral and spelling it out in margin
         with a line drawn to its position
      D. drawing a square around the numeral

8. In make-up, pages are laid out on   8.__
      A. dummies   B. folios   C. plan sheets   D. proof sheets

9. Type size is measured   9.__
      A. ems   B. inches   C. picas   D. points

10. A pica is   10.__
      A. just over 1/6 of an inch   B. just under 1/6 of an inch
      C. 1/72 of an inch   D. none of the above

11. Columns are measured in   11.__
      A. ems   B. fractions of a page
      C. picas   D. points

12. 36 points is   12.__
      A. about an inch   B. about half an inch
      C. about two inches   D. none of the foregoing

13. Copy marked to be set *ff* means to make type   13.__
      A. larger   B. smaller   C. thicker   D. thinner

14. The letters in italic type   14.__
      A. are less cursive than in roman type
      B. are more formal than in roman type
      C. are set by hand
      D. slant bottom left to top right

15. Sans-serif type   15.__
      A. has no additional fonts
      B. has no curlicues
      C. has not hangers or risers
      D. is old-fashioned German type

Questions 16-20

DIRECTIONS: Questions 16 through 20 consist of groups of four
            words.
            Select answer A if only ONE word is spelled correctly
            in a group.
            Select answer B if   TWO words are spelled correctly
            in a group.
            Select answer C if THREE words are spelled correctly
            in a group.
            Select answer D if all FOUR words are spelled correctly
            in a group.

16. counterfeit   embarass   panicky   supercede   16.__

17.	benefited	personnel	questionnaire	unparalelled	17.___
18.	bankruptcy	describable	proceed	vacuum	18.___
19.	handicapped	mispell	offerred	pilgrimmage	19.___
20.	corduroy	interfere	privilege	separator	20.___

Questions 21 - 25

DIRECTIONS: For each question numbered 21 through 25, select the
option whose meaning is MOST NEARLY the same as that
of the numbered item.

21. CONDONE   21.___
    A. complete   B. condemn   C. cooperate   D. pardon

22. EXTENUATE   22.___
    A. accuse   B. excuse   C. lengthen   D. narrow

23. MORDANT   23.___
    A. caustic   B. depressed   C. dying   D. unwholesome

24. SPATE   24.___
    A. broad road   B. excessive quantity
    C. fish eggs   D. mineral springs

25. TORTUOUS   25.___
    A. devious   B. foul   C. injurious   D. painful

_____

KEY (CORRECT ANSWERS)

1. C		11. C	
2. A		12. B	
3. A		13. C	
4. B		14. D	
5. C		15. B	
6. A		16. B	
7. A		17. C	
8. A		18. D	
9. D		19. A	
10. B		20. D	

21. D
22. B
23. A
24. B
25. A

_____

TEST 2

DIRECTIONS: Each question or incomplete statement is followed by several suggested answers or completions. Select the one that *BEST* answers the question or completes the statement. *PRINT THE LETTER OF THE CORRECT ANSWER IN THE SPACE AT THE RIGHT.*

1. Of the following, the PRINCIPAL reason why most employee house magazines are sent by mail rather than delivered at the plant is to
    A. reach the families of employees
    B. reduce personnel needed to distribute magazines
    C. shorten time involved in distributing magazines
    D. take advantage of the low mailing rates

1.___

2. Press releases received by a newspaper are usually directed to the
    A. city editor   B. managing editor
    C. promotion Manager   D. publisher

2.___

3. The agency of the United States Government that supervises radio and television broadcasting is known by the abbreviation
    A. ABC   B. FCC   C. FTC   D. SEC

3.___

4. The names of the sports editors of all state daily newspapers would be found in
    A. ADVERTISING AGE
    B. Ayer's DIRECTORY OF PERIODICALS
    C. EDITOR AND PUBLISHER INTERNATIONAL YEARBOOK
    D. PUBLIC AFFAIRS INFORMATION JOURNAL

4.___

5. Of the following, the type of publicity MOST likely to promote morale of the employees of your department would be a(n)
    A. article concerning the department written for a technical publication
    B. article in the annual report summarizing the activities of the department
    C. local newspaper article on the accomplishments of the employees of the agency
    D. short *oddity* on your superior carried by AP

5.___

6. If you wanted one photograph of a street accident to illustrate the need for improving traffic control at the scene of the accident, you should select a picture that shows
    A. a close-up of the cars and the victim
    B. a policeman questioning witnesses at the accident scenes
    C. the cars and the victim against the whole intersection of the accident scene
    D. the victim being put into an ambulance

6.___

7. The one of the following which is NOT a miniature camera is the
   A. Nikon   B. Contax   C. Leica   D. Rolleiflex

7.___

8. To mortise a cut is to
   A. cut out a portion for inclusion of type
   B. get it level with surrounding slugs of type
   C. return it to engravers for corrections
   D. send it to the morgue

8.___

9. A picture known as *cheesecake* is an example of
   A. a *mug* shot   B. a scenic shot
   C. facsimile reproduction   D. *leg* art

9.___

10. A *mat* of a picture is a
    A. copy negative
    B. papier mache impression from which plate may be cast
    C. picture page dummy from which copies are made
    D. print on dull finish paper

10.___

Questions 11 - 20

DIRECTIONS: In questions 11 through 20, print on your answer sheet, next to the corresponding question number, the capital letter immediately preceding the word or phrase which is CLOSEST in meaning to that of the capitalized letter.

11. BIBLIOPHILE
    A. appendix   B. library
    C. list of references   D. lover of books

11.___

12. SACERDOTAL
    A. penitential   B. priestly   C. reminiscent   D. spirtual

12.___

13. FLAGELLATE
    A. communicate by signals   B. pillage
    C. play the flute   D. scourge

13.___

14. SAGA
    A. epoch   B. hero   C. inscription   D. legend

14.___

15. APOCRYPHAL
    A. annotated   B. orthodox   C. unauthentic   D. visionary

15.___

16. CAVIL
    A. make captious objection   B. punish severely
    C. render just praise   D. warn emphatically

16.___

17. SHIBBOLETH
    A. seventh year   B. stone block
    C. watchword   D. weapon

17._

18. ARRANT   18.__
    A. deceitful   B. notorious   C. overbearing   D. parched

19. RUE   19.__
    A. abandon   B. despair   C. repent   D. stain

20. MORDANT   20.__
    A. caustic   B. depressed   C. dying   D. unwholesome

Questions 21 - 25

DIRECTIONS: Each question or incomplete statement is followed
               by several suggested answers or completions. Select
               the one that *BEST* answers the questions or completes
               the statement. *PRINT THE LETTER OF THE CORRECT
               ANSWER IN THE SPACE AT THE RIGHT.*

21. Of the following, the grammatically CORRECT sentence is: 21.__
    A. Neither the mayor nor the city clerk are willing
       to talk.
    B. Neither the mayor nor the city clerk is willing to
       talk.
    C. Neither the mayor or the city clerk are willing to
       to talk.
    D. Neither the mayor or the city clerk is willing to
       talk.

22. Of the following, the grammatically CORRECT sentence is: 22.__
    A. Being that he is that kind of boy, cooperation cannot
       be expected.
    B. He interviewed people who he thought had something to
       say.
    C. Stop whomever enters the building regardless of rank or
       office held.
    D. Passing through the countryside, the scenery pleased us.

23. Of the following, the grammatically CORRECT sentence is: 23.__
    A. The childrens' shoes were in their closet.
    B. The children's shoes were in their closet.
    C. The childs' shoes were in their closet.
    D. The childs' shoes were in his closet.

24. Of the following, the grammatically INCORRECT sentence is: 24.__
    A. Dissatisfaction with the theoretical bases and practical
       workings of the general property tax has given rise to
       two movements of tax reform.
    B. Let the book lie on the table.
    C. Since the department is reducing its number of employees
       is not proof that they are not needed.
    D. Who do you think will be selected for the position?

25. Of the following, the grammatically INCORRECT sentence is: 25.____
   A. Application of the principles discovered during those experiments have been of great value to mankind.
   B. Every one of the editorial assistants proved his worth without exception.
   C. State regulation of morals aids in the protection of the family.
   D. Working when one is tired does not yield the best results.

KEY (CORRECT ANSWERS)

1.	A	11.	D
2.	A	12.	B
3.	B	13.	D
4.	C	14.	D
5.	C	15.	C
6.	C	16.	A
7.	D	17.	C
8.	A	18.	B
9.	D	19.	C
10.	B	20.	A

21.	B
22.	B
23.	B
24.	C
25.	A

EXAMINATION SECTION

TEST 1

DIRECTIONS: Each question or incomplete statement is followed by several suggested answers or completions. Select the one that BEST answers the question or completes the statement. *PRINT THE LETTER OF THE CORRECT ANSWER IN THE SPACE AT THE RIGHT.*

1. An unscreened engraving is called   1.___
   A. a half-tone   B. a line cut
   C. a mat   D. copper plate

2. You are to illustrate an article with a map that still   2.___
   must be drawn.
   For layout purposes, it is desirable to
   A. ask artist to draw map to fit space available in your
      layout
   B. hold up layout until map is drawn
   C. hold up layout until map is engraved
   D. lay out page, making engraving fit space available

3. Benday process is a means of   3.___
   A. adding a second color
   B. engraving on plastic
   C. printing without plates
   D. putting shading in line cuts

4. Engravings become sharper if the art from which they are   4.___
   made is
   A. black ink on grey paper
   B. larger than engraving size
   C. plastic coated
   D. smaller than engraving size

5. For layout purposes, it is sometimes desirable to *flop* a   5.___
   cut.
   This CANNOT be done if the
   A. art is to be reduced
   B. engraving is to be made speedily
   C. engraving contains printing
   D. engraving is not rectangular

6. A picture 7½" wide and 13½" deep is to be made into an   6.___
   engraving for a page with 2½" columns.
   How deep will a two-column cut be?
   A. 8"   B. 8½"   C. 9"   D. 9½"

7. Social scientists have found that when emotional tensions   7.___
   are aroused,
   A. people listen more intently and the message makes a
      greater impact
   B. people react immediately and the *pitch* should be made
      quickly

    C. tendencies toward distraction are increased and the
       attention function is temporarily impaired
    D. the message has the greatest chance of reaching *home*

8. Public relations experts say that MAXIMUM effect for a 8._
   message results from
    A. concentrating in one medium
    B. ignoring mass media and concentrating on *opinion makers*
    C. presenting only those factors which support a given
       position
    D. using a combination of two or more of the available
       media

9. To assure credibility and avoid hostility, the public 9._
   relations man MUST
    A. make certain his message is truthful, not evasive or
       exaggerated
    B. make sure his message contains some dire consequence,
       if ignored
    C. repeat the message often enough so that it cannot be
       ignored
    D. try to reach as many people and groups as possible

10. The public relations man MUST be prepared to assume that 10._
    members of his audience
    A. may have developed attitudes toward his proposals -
       favorable, neutral, or unfavorable
    B. will be immediately hostile
    C. will consider his proposals with an open mind
    D. will invariably need an introduction to his subject

11. To a copy editor, *slug* means 11._
    A. first sentence of story
    B. identification of story
    C. size of type in which story is to be set
    D. story needs punch or drive

12. The usual way to *count* type in writing headlines is by 12._
    A. caps and lowercase   B. measurement
    C. the *stick*   D. units

13. Wire service teletype copy USUALLY 13._
    A. can be sent directly to the composing room
    B. has not been copy-edited
    C. needs careful scrutiny to avoid libel suits
    D. requires capitalization

14. The lead is the MOST important part of a news story. 14._
    It should
    A. attract the reader
    B. give all the facts immediately
    C. start with the source of the story
    D. start with the time of the story

15. There are several acceptable ways of writing a news story. 15.___
    It should USUALLY be written
    A. as facts become known, regardless of chronology
    B. chronologically
    C. in order of decreasing importance or interest
    D. so that details come at the end

16. A reporter assigned to cover a scheduled broadcast speech 16.___
    GENERALLY
    A. gets shorthand notes afterwards
    B. takes shorthand notes himself
    C. receives an advance copy
    D. writes his story from the radio or television broadcast

17. A reporter is told that an interview has been set up for 17.___
    him for the next day with an authority on earthquakes.
    He is given the name and affiliation of the authority
    and the location and time of the interview.
    His NEXT step is to
    A. bring along a seismology expert to the interview
    B. do research on seismology in an encyclopedia and get
       biographical data on interviewee
    C. try to arrange a luncheon date with interviewee
    D. verify time and place of interview

18. When a story is worth handling on a continuing basis, 18.___
    even if no added news is available, a writer will be
    asked to
    A. call the sources on deadline and make sure no facts
       are changed
    B. rearrange the story, putting other details in the lead
    C. shorten the story
    D. write a *second day* lead

19. There are almost as many techniques of interviewing as 19.___
    there are interviewers.
    Of the following, the LEAST objectionable method is to
    A. ask if interviewee minds being quoted
    B. make occasional notes as important topics come up
    C. take notes unobtrusively
    D. take shorthand notes of every word

20. There are many differences between feature and news 20.___
    stories.
    The single MOST important difference is that
    A. features are longer than news stories
    B. features emphasize the unusual; news stories the
       significant
    C. features ignore facts that news stories cannot
    D. news stories are more timely than features

Questions 21-25.

DIRECTIONS: In each of Questions 21 through 25, only one of the four sentences conforms to standards of correct usage. The other three contain errors in grammar, diction, or punctuation. Select the option in each question which conforms to standards of correct usage. Consider an option correct if it contains none of the errors mentioned above, even though there may be other correct ways of expressing the same thought.

21. A. Because he was ill was no excuse for his behavior.   21.__
     B. I insist that he see a lawyer before he goes to trial.
     C. He said "that he had not intended to go."
     D. He wasn't out of the office only three days.

22. A. He came to the station and pays a porter to carry his   22.__
        bags into the train.
     B. I should have liked to live in medieval times.
     C. My father was born in Linville. A little country town
        where everyone knows everyone else.
     D. The car, which is parked across the street, is disabled.

23. A. He asked the desk clerk for a clean, quiet, room.   23.__
     B. I expected James to be lonesome and that he would want
        to go home.
     C. I have stopped worrying because I have heard nothing
        further on the subject.
     D. If the board of directors controls the company, they
        may take actions which are disapproved by the stock-
        holders.

24. A. Each of the players knew their place.   24.__
     B. He whom you saw on the stage is the son of an actor.
     C. Susan is the smartest of the twin sisters.
     D. Who ever thought of him winning both prizes?

25. A. An outstanding trait of early man was their reliance   25.__
        on omens.
     B. Because I had never been there before.
     C. Neither Mr. Jones nor Mr. Smith has completed his work.
     D. While eating my dinner, a dog came to the window.

KEY (CORRECT ANSWERS)

1. B	6. C	11. B	16. C	21. B
2. B	7. C	12. D	17. B	22. B
3. D	8. D	13. D	18. D	23. C
4. B	9. A	14. A	19. C	24. B
5. C	10. A	15. C	20. B	25. C

TEST 2

DIRECTIONS: Each question or incomplete statement is followed by several suggested answers or completions. Select the one that BEST answers the question or completes the statement. *PRINT THE LETTER OF THE CORRECT ANSWER IN THE SPACE AT THE RIGHT.*

1. Last minute editorial changes by the editor after the text has been set are MOST likely to be marked
   A. AA   B. ATF   C. HFC   D. PE

   1.___

2. The term *double truck* is used to describe
   A. a two column headline
   B. the first page of the second section
   C. two adjacent pages made up as one
   D. two pictures combined into a single picture

   2.___

3. Acknowledgment of a borrowed cut is made by means of a(n)
   A. credit line   B. dingbat
   C. overline   D. runover

   3.___

4. The printer of a monthly publication is expected to keep available for possible future use, without storage charges or special instructions,
   A. gravure copper printing plates
   B. letterpress plates
   C. offset plates
   D. rotogravure printing cylinders

   4.___

5. The terms *linotype* and *intertype* refer to
   A. kinds of typewriters   B. proof-taking machines
   C. slug casting machines   D. types of presses

   5.___

6. The technique of estimating the dimensions of an engraving which will be made from a picture is known as
   A. casting off   B. cropping
   C. routing   D. scaling down

   6.___

7. Of the following, the screen ruling used MOST frequently for reproducing photographs on newsprint is _____-line.
   A. 65   B. 100   C. 120   D. 240

   7.___

8. If the manuscript for a publication could fill 53 printed pages, but you were restricted to the following choices, the MOST economical and efficient procedure would be to _____ to _____ pages.
   A. cut; 46   B. cut; 48
   C. cut; 50   D. expand; 54

   8.___

9. In typography, the number of points to an inch is APPROXIMATELY
   A. 12   B. 48   C. 72   D. 96

   9.___

10. All variants of a particular type design are said to   10._
    belong to the same
    A. family   B. font   C. quad   D. run

11. Old English is in a class of type known as   11._
    A. black letter   B. italic
    C. roman   D. script

12. The type called sans-serif is also known as   12._
    A. baskerville   B. bodoni
    C. gothic   D. roman

13. The one of the following which is NOT a principal kind of   13._
    type is
    A. italic   B. monotype   C. script   D. text

14. Of the following, the preferred process for obtaining   14._
    1,000 copies of material containing photographs is
    A. electrotype   B. letter press
    C. offset   D. rotogravure

15. The one of the following terms which does NOT apply to   15._
    headlines is
    A. bank   B. bulldog   C. dropline   D. spread

16. A method of printing in which a relief process is used is   16._
    A. intaglio   B. letter press
    C. lithography   D. offset

17. A screened engraving of a photograph is known as a   17._
    A. intaglio   B. letter press
    C. lithography   D. offset

18. In typography, the term used for arranging type in lines   18._
    so that all the lines in a column are even is
    A. conversion   B. furnishing
    C. justifying   D. leading

19. The front page of THE NEW YORK TIMES most frequently   19._
    exemplifies the make-up known as
    A. balanced   B. circus
    C. focus   D. hanging indentation

20. Excellence in newspaper make-up is annually recognized by   20._
    the presentation of the
    A. Adolph S. Ochs Trophy
    B. F. Wayland Ayer Cup
    C. George Polk Memorial Award
    D. Silurian Society Cup

21. The word *stet* tells the printer to   21._
    A. capitalize all letters in the phrase
    B. omit the phrase
    C. reinstate the phrase marked out
    D. set the marked phrase in italics

22. In proofreading, the symbol ✓✓✓ indicates that the printer should   22.___
    A. check with original manuscript
    B. correct faulty spacing
    C. insert quotation marks
    D. straighten lines

23. A proofreader indicates a *bad* or defective letter by the symbol   23.___

    A. ✗   B. ▭   C. ↯   D. ♯

24. The proofreading symbol meaning *close up partly but leave some space* is   24.___

    A. (/)   B. ⊙   C. ♯   D. ▭

25. A proof containing the misspelling *Beleive* should be marked   25.___

    A. tr   B. wf   C. ⊙   D. ⌐

———

KEY (CORRECT ANSWERS)

1. A
2. C
3. A
4. A
5. C

6. D
7. A
8. B
9. C
10. A

11. A
12. C
13. B
14. C
15. B

16. B
17. A
18. C
19. A
20. B

21. C
22. B
23. A
24. C
25. A

———

EXAMINATION SECTION
TEST 1

DIRECTIONS: Each question or incomplete statement is followed by
several suggested answers or completions. Select the
one that BEST answers the question or completes the
statement. *PRINT THE LETTER OF THE CORRECT ANSWER IN
THE SPACE AT THE RIGHT.*

1. Of the following, the order in which a piece of local copy   1.___
    is MOST likely to flow is
       A. city editor, copy reader, compositor
       B. compositor, city editor, copy reader
       C. compositor, copy reader, city editor
       D. copy reader, compositor, city editor

2. The one who edits copy and writes headlines at a newspaper   2.___
    copy desk is USUALLY called a
       A. copy cutter   B. copy holder
       C. rim man   D. slot man

3. Of the following, a comprehensive single-volume reference   3.___
    book for general information is
       A. FACTS ON FILE
       B. the CONGRESSIONAL DIRECTORY
       C. the STATISTICAL ABSTRACT OF THE UNITED STATES GOVERN-
          MENT
       D. the WORLD ALMANAC

4. As a defense against libel, one could claim that a state-   4.___
    ment was quoted from the CONGRESSIONAL RECORD and, there-
    fore, was a(n)
       A. indirect quotation   B. personal comment
       C. privileged statement   D. reporter's prerogative

5. In order to have an illustration continue off the edge of   5.___
    a page, you would instruct the printer to
       A. bleed   B. cutoff   C. justify   D. mortise

6. The description which accompanies a photograph or diagram   6.___
    is called a(n)
       A. caption   B. flag
       C. overhead   D. underhead

7. A headline stretching across all columns of a page is   7.___
    called a
       A. bank   B. banner
       C. cross line   D. drop line

8. You would expect a headline that is flush right and left   8.___
    to
       A. comprise two or more decks
       B. fill the entire line

C. have black em borders at both ends
D. have two ems of white space on both left and right hand sides

9. A headline that carries a story continued from another page is known as a
   A. break   B. filler   C. jump   D. read-in

9.___

10. The secondary part of a headline is a
    A. byline   B. deck   C. slug   D. subhead

10.___

11. A single piece of type that includes two or more letters is called
    A. dingbat   B. linotype
    C. logotype   D. nonpareil

11.___

12. The one of the following terms which indicates that type is jumbled and no longer of use is
    A. fudge   B. mash   C. montage   D. pi

12.___

13. Type left over and unused after a magazine has been sent to press is called
    A. folo copy   B. make-ready
    C. overset   D. quoin

13.___

14. An upper and lower case crossline reads as follows: Dr. Doe Appointed. The unit count of this crossline is
    A. 14½   B. 16   C. 18   D. 19

14.___

15. An incomplete story consists of the following parts:
    First add, first add insert, insert after first add, lead, precede, second add.
    An additional piece of copy marked *second add insert* is added to complete the story.
    In the final sequence of the completed story, this piece of copy would appear as the _____ item.
    A. second   B. fourth   C. fifth   D. sixth

15.___

16. When copy for a standard-size newspaper is returned with instructions to *cut to 1 col.*, the number of words should be reduced to APPROXIMATELY
    A. 500   B. 1000   C. 1500   D. 2000

16.___

17. In copyreading, two straight lines placed under a word indicates that it should be set in
    A. boldface   B. capitals and lower case
    C. italics   D. small capitals

17.___

18. When a story is continued on a second page, the copyreader marks the bottom of the first page with
    A. ##   B. -30-   C. insuff.   D. more

18.___

19. The copyreader's symbol which is used to indicate that a   19.___
    subhead should be centered is

A. ⌞   B. ⌟   C. ⅃L   D. ⌐

20. The copyreader's symbol which is used to indicate the   20.___
    start of a paragraph is

A. ⌞   B. #   C. ◯   D. ∼

Questions 21-25.

DIRECTIONS: Questions 21 through 25 consist of four pairs of words
             each. Some of the words are spelled correctly; others
             are spelled incorrectly. For each question, indicate
             in the space at the right the letter preceding that
             pair of words in which BOTH words are spelled CORRECTLY.

21. A. hygienic, inviegle   B. omniscience, pittance   21.___
     C. plagarize, nullify   D. seargent, perilous

22. A. auxilary, existence   B. pronounciation, accordance 22.___
     C. ignominy, indegence   D. suable, baccalaureate

23. A. discreet, inaudible   B. hypocrisy, currupt   23.___
     C. liquidate, maintainance   D. transparancy, onerous

24. A. facility, stimulent   B. frugel, sanitary   24.___
     C. monetary, prefatory   D. punctileous, credentials

25. A. bankruptsy, perceptible   B. disuade, resilient   25.___
     C. exhilerate, expectancy   D. panegyric, disparate

___

KEY (CORRECT ANSWERS)

1. A		11. C	
2. C		12. D	
3. D		13. C	
4. C		14. B	
5. A		15. D	
6. A		16. B	
7. B		17. D	
8. B		18. D	
9. C		19. C	
10. B		20. A	

21. B
22. D
23. A
24. C
25. D

___

TEST 2

DIRECTIONS: Each question or incomplete statement is followed by several suggested answers or completions. Select the one that BEST answers the question or completes the statement. *PRINT THE LETTER OF THE CORRECT ANSWER IN THE SPACE AT THE RIGHT.*

1. Spot news stories are USUALLY written   1.____
   A. as feature articles
   B. in inverted pyramid style
   C. to fill inside pages
   D. with chronological organization

2. The Flesch formula is concerned with   2.____
   A. body type size
   B. front page make-up
   C. headline styles
   D. sentence length and number of syllables

3. A good reporter avoids taking extensive notes during an   3.____
   interview because
   A. accuracy is of secondary importance in reporting an
      interview
   B. a rewrite man may actually write the story
   C. this may mark the reporter as an amateur
   D. this may distract the person being interviewed

4. A reporter is present at a function where a distinguished   4.____
   person is scheduled to speak. He has a complete advance
   copy of the text.
   During the speech, the reporter could BEST use his time to
   A. follow the text to see if the speaker deviates from
      it
   B. organize the material of the text for later writing
   C. take direct quotations from the text
   D. write headlines for the story

5. A news story written in an inverted pyramid form is one   5.____
   in which the
   A. climax is reached at the end of the story
   B. climax is reached near the middle of the story
   C. facts are arranged in chronological order of occur-
      rence
   D. facts are arranged in descending order of reader
      interest

6. In a news story, the first mention of the former Catholic   6.____
   Cardinal of New York should be written as
   A. Cardinal Terence Cook
   B. Terence Cardinal Cook
   C. The Rt. Rev. Terence Cook
   D. The Very Rev. Terence Cook

7. The second reference to the British statesman in a news-
   paper story should be written as   7.___
   A. Lord Churchill   B. Mr. Churchill
   C. Sir Churchill   D. Sir Winston

8. The MOST common type of lead on newspaper stories is the   8.___
   _____ lead.
   A. astonisher   B. quotation
   C. summary   D. suspended-interest

9. The one of the following terms which does NOT designate   9.___
   a story accompanying a report of a major news event is
   A. precede   B. shirt tail
   C. sidebar   D. subhead

10. A second day story is also known as a   10.___
    A. filler   B. flimsy
    C. follow copy   D. follow story

11. A phrase or word used on copy to identify additional   11.___
    pages of a news story is called a
    A. headline   B. slot   C. slug   D. stamp

12. A *tear sheet* is a   12.___
    A. carbon copy of a story
    B. galley proof of a story
    C. page proof of a publication
    D. printed page from a publication

13. If you were told to *boil* a story, you would   13.___
    A. expand with editorial comment
    B. present only essential facts
    C. try to keep it a *scoop*
    D. write a large headline spread

14. If a reporter went to the *morgue*, he would be seeking   14.___
    A. carbon copies of an article he had just written
    B. clippings on the subject he was writing about
    C. galley proofs of a recently completed article
    D. incoming press association teletype copy

15. A beat reporter's *future book* is a   15.___
    A. chronological listing of expected events on his beat
    B. list of news sources on his beat
    C. novel he eventually hopes to write
    D. schedule of assignments kept for editor of editorial
       page

16. To a magazine editor, the term *query* means a   16.___
    A. letter outlining an article idea
    B. personal request for conference with the editor
    C. request for an advance
    D. rough draft of an article

17. The one of the following who is NOT on the editorial staff   17.___
    of a large metropolitan newspaper is the
    A. copyreader   B. photographer
    C. proofreader   D. rewrite man

18. The conventional name given to a staff member who   18.___
    gathers news on a daily paper and telephones into the
    office is
    A. bulldog   B. cub   C. leg man   D. slot man

19. Material for future release would probably be marked   19.___
    A. F.Y.I.   B. H.F.R.   C. H.T.K.   D. M.E.

20. When a reporter sends a news item by telegraph from out   20.___
    of town at night, he MOST probably would mark it
    A. BOM   B. DPR   C. EOS   D. NPR

21. Of the following newspapers, the one with the LARGEST   21.___
    circulation is the
    A. CHICAGO TRIBUNE   B. NEW YORK DAILY NEWS
    C. NEW YORK TIMES   D. PHILADELPHIA BULLETIN

22. Copyrighted material in the United States can be protected   22.___
    for a MAXIMUM of _____ years.
    A. 16   B. 42   C. 56   D. 99

23. Of the following, the BEST source of biographical infor-   23.___
    mation on a famous living American sociologist is
    A. the COLUMBIA ENCYCLOPEDIA
    B. the DICTIONARY OF AMERICAN BIOGRAPHY
    C. the NATIONAL BIOGRAPHICAL INDEX
    D. WHO'S WHO IN AMERICA

24. A book's index is USUALLY prepared from   24.___
    A. dummy sheets   B. edited copy
    C. galley proof   D. page proof

25. If you desire to include copyrighted material amounting   25.___
    to well over 2,000 words in an article, you should obtain
    written permission from the
    A. author
    B. copyright holder
    C. Library of Congress copyright office
    D. publisher

———

KEY (CORRECT ANSWERS)

1. B	6. B	11. C	16. A	21. B
2. D	7. D	12. D	17. C	22. C
3. D	8. C	13. B	18. C	23. D
4. A	9. D	14. B	19. B	24. D
5. D	10. D	15. A	20. D	25. B

———

EXAMINATION SECTION

TEST 1

DIRECTIONS: Each question or incomplete statement is followed by several suggested answers or completions. Select the one that BEST answers the question or completes the statement. *PRINT THE LETTER OF THE CORRECT ANSWER IN THE SPACE AT THE RIGHT.*

1. You are preparing a press release announcing a corner-   1.____
   stone laying ceremony for a housing project named after
   a prominent New Yorker. You desire to include in this
   press release some information about this person's contributions to public housing.
   Of the following sources which are available to you, the
   BEST one to go to in order to obtain this information is
       A. the index and issues of a local newpaper obtainable
          in the public library
       B. the World Almanac
       C. a book on the history of public housing
       D. a biography of the individual

2. You have been assigned to prepare a press release announc-   2.____
   ing the issuance of applications for apartments at a new
   city housing project. Of the following items of information,
   the one which it is LEAST important to include in such a
   press release is the
       A. average cost per apartment
       B. rental charges per room
       C. number of apartments in the project
       D. special facilities available at the project

3. The chairman of the housing authority has asked you to   3.____
   assist him in preparing a speech he is to deliver at the
   ground-breaking ceremonies for the Authority's 100th per-
   manent housing project. Members of the city, state and
   federal administrations will be present, as well as the
   press and the general public.
   Of the following, the theme which you should emphasize
   most in this speech is the
       A. role of the chairman in expediting housing progress
       B. failure of private industry to provide for the housing
          needs of low-income families
       C. steady march toward the elimination of the city's slums
       D. benefits of living in a democracy

4. You have been assigned to prepare an information brochure   4.____
   which is to be distributed to public welfare clients. After
   preliminary study you find that the value of this brochure
   will be greatly increased if it is prepared in such a way as
   to include several pictorial illustrations. You do not have
   the skill necessary to prepare these illustrations.
   Of the following, the *best* action for you to take is to
       A. prepare the brochure in such a manner as not to require
          illustrations
       B. ask another employee, who can do the illustrations, to
          assist you by doing the illustrations

    C. prepare the brochure with such illustrations as you
       are able to draw
    D. find out first whether someone will be available to do
       the illustrations for you

5. The deputy commissioner of the Department of Welfare has   5.____
asked you to assist him in preparing a speech. The deputy
commissioner is to represent the department as the guest of
honor at a banquet given by a civic organization.
Of the following, the *most desirable* action for you to take
before beginning to write this speech is to
    A. consult the civic organization to secure background
       material
    B. arrange for a brief conference with the deputy commissioner
       in order to determine his wishes as to the general tone
       and content of the speech
    C. secure a copy of a speech delivered on a similar previous
       occasion and closely model your speech after it
    D. find out whether the speech will be broadcast

6. Of the following, it is generally *most desirable* that   6.____
informational material written for reading by public welfare
clients be
    A. brief and concise
    B. easily understood
    C. couched in correct technical terms
    D. easy to translate into foreign languages

7. Suppose that you are assigned to release department infor-   7.____
mation to reporters for the metropolitan press. Of the
following, the LEAST desirable practice for you to adopt
in this assignment is
    A. as a general rule, release information in written form
       only
    B. set regular dates for the release of department news
       insofar as possible
    C. secure clearance for the issuance of all written releases
    D. release information first to reporters for newspapers
       which give the best coverage to department news

8. A letter from a private citizen, complaining about a de-   8.____
partment policy which has worked a hardship on him, has
been referred to you for reply. The citizen asks that this
policy be changed.
In answering this letter, it would be *best* to give major
emphasis to
    A. an explanation of the reasons which make such a policy
       necessary
    B. pointing out that the department regulations cannot be
       revised to suit each individual case
    C. stating that the operations of any large organization
       must result in some hardships
    D. inducing the individual to come into the office where the
       matter can better be dealt with in a face-to-face interview

9. Suppose you are assigned to prepare the annual report for your department. Each bureau has been asked to submit a written report on its activities for the preceding year. Of the following, the *most desirable* action for you to take in carrying out this assignment is to

9.____

    A. return to the bureau heads for revision those reports which, in your opinion, contain unimportant material

    B. rewrite the material submitted by the bureaus to secure improved style without changing content

    C. arrange a conference with the bureau heads to discuss the reports they are to submit

    D. write an introduction and conclusion and let the reports of the bureaus constitute, unaltered, the body of the annual report

10. You have been assigned by your supervisor to do the preliminary editing of material written by other information assistants. After a week in this assignment you evaluate the material submitted by one information assistant as of lower quality than that of the others. Of the following, the *best* action for you to take is to

10.____

    A. analyze his work with the other information assistants

    B. continue to edit his work without comment at this time

    C. suggest to him that he take a refresher course in writing

    D. recommend his transfer to less original work

11. You have completed gathering the necessary data for a routine newspaper release you are to write. The *most desirable* step for you to take next is to

11.____

    A. write a first draft of the release

    B. work out a plan for the release, including the beginning, the main points, and the ending

    C. develop a suitable title and then begin to write

    D. have someone familiar with the field check the accuracy of the data which you have gathered

12. Of the following writing techniques, the one which is generally LEAST effective for making written matter more forceful is the

12.____

    A. repetition of a key word or phrase

    B. liberal use of exclamation points, capitalization, underlining, and other similar devices

    C. use of the verbs in the active voice, rather than the passive voice

    D. use of a brief sentence, rather than a longer one, to express the same idea

13. The use of anecdotes and other verbal illustrations in writing is desirable *primarily* because

13.____

    A. this is a good way of showing the author's interest in his subject

    B. the reader will remember the anecdotes

    C. the illustrations will help the reader to remember the author's main idea

    D. the illustrations will entertain the reader

14. The technique of directly addressing the reader of a novel 14.____
    or short story
    A. has been gaining favor steadily during recent years
    B. has been the prevailing practice for a long time
    C. is more common in popular fiction than in literary
       fiction
    D. is considered out-of-date today

15. The one of the following which is considered LEAST im- 15.____
    portant is good newswriting is
    A. complete accuracy of names and addresses
    B. full identification of sources of information
    C. strict chronological order of presentation
    D. avoiding the use of editorial statements

16. Of the following, the *best* procedure to follow when 16.____
    writing an article to be read by experts is to
    A. avoid the technical terms as far as possible
    B. explain the technical terms the first time they
       are used
    C. use the technical terms of the experts
    D. use your literary judgment as to whether to use the
       technical terms

17. Of the following, the purpose for which it is LEAST 17.____
    important for a writer to have a large vocabulary is to
    A. give him a wider choice of synonyms and antonyms
    B. enable him to express himself in a sophisticated
       language
    C. improve his reading comprehension
    D. make his writing more exact

18. "The family lived in a small edifice on Maple Street." 18.____
    The preceding sentence involves a
    A. good choice of words
    B. poor choice of words because an "edifice" is large
       rather than small
    C. poor choice of words because the word "edifice" is
       obsolete
    D. poor choice of words because the word "edifice" is
       unfamiliar to the average reader

19. In fiction, the *best* way of acquainting the reader with 19.____
    the traits of the characters is through
    A. action
    B. dialogue and description
    C. action and dialogue
    D. dialogue

20. Subheads in an informal pamphlet 20.____
    A. are a matter of individual preference
    B. are appropriate *only* if the subject readily breaks
       itself down into separate sections
    C. should be used because the pamphlet will be easier to read
    D. should NOT be used because they look "textbookish"

21. The length of an average paragraph should 21.____
    A. be about 300 words
    B. harmonize with other elements of a writer's style
    C. not fall below 60 words
    D. vary according to each writing assignment

22. In writing for today's readers, the one of the following 22.____
    which would be LEAST suitable as a literary model for
    imitation is
    A. Abraham Lincoln   B. Samuel Johnson
    C. Mark Twain   C. Benjamin Franklin

23. Fictitious characters in factual writing should 23.____
    A. be disguised to make them appear real
    B. be given names rather than symbols
    C. be given symbols, such as A, B, and C, rather than names
    D. not be used

24. "Cliches should be **avoided** in writing." The one of the 24.____
    following which is NOT a cliche is
    A. "every Tom, Dick, and Harry"
    B. "left no stone unturned"
    C. "outrageous possibilities"
    D. "strike while the iron is hot"

25. Recent polls of the general public indicate that from 25.____
    20% to 80% of the American people are unacquainted with
    such items of general information as the United Nations
    and the Marshall plan. Of the following, the *most probable*
    cause for this lack of knowledge is that
    A. people generally don't read enough to grasp this
       information
    B. most people don't know anything about current events
       or international relations
    C. the schools avoid the teaching of controversial subjects
    D. this news was not dealt with in the newspapers read by
       the people polled

26. The "Readers' Guide to Periodical Literature" is 26.____
    A. a digest of magazine articles
    B. a literary magazine
    C. an index of magazine articles
    D. an annual guide to magazine

27. Of the following metropolitan newspapers, the one which 27.____
    has the largest daily circulation is the
    A. Daily News   B. Newsday
    C. New York Times   D. New York Post

28. The cost-of-living index is computed by the 28.____
    A. Bureau of Internal Revenue
    B. Bureau of Labor Statistics
    C. Federal Security Agency
    D. National Bureau of Standards

29. The trend revealed by the U.S. census with regard to the   29.____
    population of metropolitan areas may *best* be described as
    one of
       A. little change
       B. marked decline
       C. sharp growth
       D. shift from the center to the suburbs

30. In the United States, agreements that prohibit or restrict 30.____
    the sale of real estate to particular racial groups
       A. are a very common legal practice
       B. are commonly practiced in the South
       C. were declared legal and enforceable by the U.S.
          Supreme Court
       D. were declared legally unenforceable by the U.S.
          Supreme Court

31. Of the following sentences, the one which is poorly   31.____
    written because it contains a "dangling construction" is
       A. After waiting half an hour for the bus, I remembered
          that I had no money for carfare.
       B. Having returned from our vacations, the supervisor
          made reassignments.
       C. Smiling pleasantly, she acknowledged the applause of
          the audience.
       D. Walking over to him, I introduced myself and offered
          to help him catch his assailant.

QUESTIONS 32-36.
Questions 32-36 consist of three sentences each. For each question
select the sentence which contains NO error in grammar or usage and
write the capital letter preceding that sentence in the correspondingl
numbered space on your answer sheet.

32. A. Be sure that everybody brings his notes to the   32.____
       conference.
    B. He looked like he meant to hit the boy.
    C. Mr. Jones is one of the clients who was chosen to
       represent the district
    D. All are incorrect

33. A. He is taller than I.   33.____
    B. I'll have nothing to do with these kind of people.
    C. The reason why he will not buy the house is because
       it is too expensive.
    D. All are incorrect

34. A. Aren't I eligible for this apartment.   34.____
    B. Have you seen him anywheres?
    C. He should of come earlier.
    D. All are incorrect

35. A. He graduated college in 1982.   35.____
    B. He hadn't but one more line to write.
    C. Who do you think is the author of this report?
    D. All are incorrect

36. A. I talked to one official, whom I knew was fully   36._____
       impartial.
    B. Everyone signed the petition but him.
    C. He proved not only to be a good student but also
       a good athlete.
    D. All are incorrect

QUESTIONS 37-40.
Questions 37-40 consist of three sentences each. For each item,
select the sentence which contains NO error in word usage and write
the capital letter preceding that sentence in the correspondingly
numbered space on your answer sheet.

37. A. Every year a large amount of tenants are admitted to   37._____
       housing projects.
    B. Henry Ford owned around a billion dollars in industrial
       equipment.
    C. He was aggravated by the child's bead behavior.
    D. All are incorrect

38. A. Before he was committed to the asylum he suffered from   38._____
       the illusion that he was Napoleon.
    B. Besides stocks, there were also bonds in the safe.
    C. We bet the other team easily.
    D. All are incorrect

39. A. Bring this report to your supervisor immediately.   39._____
    B. He set the chair down near the table.
    C. The capitol of New York is Albany.
    D. All are incorrect

40. A. He was chosen to arbitrate the dispute because every-   40._____
       one knew he would be disinterested.
    B. It is advisable to obtain the best council before making
       an important decision.
    C. Less college students are interested in teaching than
       ever before.
    D. All are incorrect   _____

KEY (CORRECT ANSWERS)

1. D	11. B	21. D	31. B
2. A	12. B	22. B	32. A
3. C	13. C	23. B	33. A
4. D	14. D	24. C	34. D
5. B	15. C	25. A	35. C
6. B	16. C	26. C	36. B
7. D	17. B	27. A	37. D
8. A	18. B	28. B	38. B
9. C	19. C	29. D	39. B
10. B	20. C	30. D	40. A

TEST 2

DIRECTIONS: Each question or incomplete statement is followed by several suggested answers or completions. Select the one that BEST answers the question or completes the statement. *PRINT THE LETTER OF THE CORRECT ANSWER IN THE SPACE AT THE RIGHT.*

1. "Study your audience and slant your writing toward it."   1.____
   Of the following, the *best* procedure to adopt in applying this principle is to
   A. estimate the intelligence of your audience and write accordingly
   B. use the simplest possible prose style
   C. write about the things you believe your audience wants to read, rather than the things you would prefer to write about
   D. write about what you want to say in the form that is most likely to appeal to your audience

2. "The first rule for giving your writing 'punch' is to take   2.____
   the most important idea and save it until the end of the sentence."
   Of the following sentences, the one which *best* illustrates this principle is:
   A. After they had notified the police, and had searched the entire neighborhood for hours, they found the little girl in the attic, sleeping peacefully.
   B. The enemy has destroyed the lives of our people, plundered our seas, ravaged our coasts, and burnt our towns.
   C. The thief had stolen the top secret report, broken open the safe, and rifled the desk.
   D. The tornado left ruin and death in its wake and tore down every building in the village.

3. "America has been built by the cooperative effort of many   3.____
   different kinds of people, working together."
   In the preceding sentence, a word or phrase which is NOT made superfluous by the use of another word or phrase of similar meaning is
   A. different   B. kinds of
   C. many   D. working together

4. "The company did so well in 1980 that, at the end of the   4.____
   year, it gave each employee a carton of cigarettes, a bottle of wine, and -- a $100 bond."
   In the preceding sentence, the dash
   A. adds more force to the words which follow
   B. detracts from the force of the words which follow
   C. is an illustration of the improper use of punctuation
   D. neither adds nor detracts from the force of the words which follow

5. A letter written by another information assistant begins   5.____
   with this sentence: "We beg to acknowledge yours of the
   23d inst." It then goes on to reply directly to the matters
   raised in the letter of the 23d.
   If you are assigned to edit this letter, the most desirable
   action of the following for you to take is to
       A. change the first sentence to read: "We beg to acknowledge
          yours of the 23d inst. and in reply wish to state that..."
       B. leave the first sentence as it is
       C. leave the first sentence unchanged but add another
          immediately following summarizing what the letter of the
          23d inquired about
       D. omit the first sentence in its entirety

6. "Write as you talk" is an axiom now widely accepted by   6.____
   newspapermen. Newspaper readers have a better chance of
   grasping the news if it is told to them simply and clearly.
   The *most direct* implication of the preceding statement is that
       A. an axiom is a statement whose truth is generally accepted
          by everyone
       B. flowery or complicated language should generally be
          avoided in newspaper reporting
       C. newspaper readers are no different from newspaper re-
          porters
       D. the use of ungrammatical constructions is sometimes
          justified in writing for the newspapers

7. "Nowadays, lack of information usually goes hand in hand   7.____
   with little education; similarly, lack of information also
   usually goes hand in hand with low income. So, if you are
   writing for people in the lower income brackets or people
   who haven't gone to college, it's a good guess that they
   won't have much background knowledge."
   The preceding statement implies *most directly* that
       A. little education has always been negatively correlated
          with little information
       B. poor people are usually not well-informed
       C. people who have not gone to college are in the lower
          income brackets
       D. writing for the poor and uneducated is more difficult
          than writing for the rich and well-educated

8. "Prices of building materials are, in the aggregate, more   8.____
   rigid than those of other commodities. Concentration of
   control over the supply of goods is frequently advanced as
   the explanation for price rigidities in general and for
   building materials in particular."
   According to the preceding statement,
       A. increased demand and concurrent fixed supply are
          frequently responsible for increased prices of building
          materials
       B. in the aggregate, the high cost of building materials
          contributes substantially to the high cost of new
          housing construction
       C. the cost of most articles is generally more flexible
          than the cost of articles required in the construction
          of new buildings
       D. the existence of faulty methods of distribution is often
          advanced as an argument to explain price inequities

9. "In undertaking a new development, the builder first de-   9.___
   cides upon the price or rental range of the dwellings he
   proposes to construct. Then, after roughly estimating the
   cost of the selected structure, he tries to find land at
   suitable prices."
   According to the preceding statement,
   A. after a new development is completed, the builder adds
      up his construction and land costs and fixes the price
      of the individual house accordingly
   B. it is difficult to predict the probable cost of a new
      dwelling unit because of constant fluctuation in the
      cost of building materials
   C. land costs influence the selling price of dwellings least
   D. the selling price of a house is usually determined
      before construction is begun

10. "A construction program initiated by public agencies better 10.___
    protects the home buyer and insures the greater soundness of
    the neighborhood."
    According to the preceding statement,
    A. a home buyer is more confident of the safety of his
       investment if he is given to understand that the
       neighborhood will not change
    B. a public agency is more responsible in construction
       programs than a private builder could hope to be
    C. since a public agency can, if necessary, control the
       development of a neighborhood through zoning laws,
       public housing is more desirable
    D. to insure the soundness of a neighborhood it is more
       effective to have the building of new homes planned
       by public agencies

11. "To achieve sound planning we cannot rely on educating   11.___
    the builder to the fact that what is good for the public
    will be ultimately good for him, for his interest is usually
    short term and the pattern in which he functions is not
    set up for voluntary reform.
    According to the preceding statement,
    A. a builder is not interest in educating the public to
       its ultimate benefits
    B. builders whose interests are usually of short duration
       can be educated to set up voluntary reforms
    C. since a builder's interest in any property is usually
       of short duration, he will voluntarily function for
       public benefit
    D. we cannot rely on educating a builder to the fact that
       public benefit is to his advantage in the long run

12. "If cities had a long range objective, if they had plans   12.___
    showing the expected line of growth, plans for their future
    schools and parks, their houses and their locations, their
    industries and their locations, their future transportation
    facilities and their utilities, then with the advent of an
    emergency requiring government spending they could channel
    the expenditures and step up the program along the lines of
    the larger long term plans."
    According to the preceding statement,
    A. a city wishing to eliminate slums can with proper planning

take advantage of an emergency requiring the channeling
of expenditures
    B. an emergency requires the channeling of expenditures
       so that greater efficiency can be shown in planning
    C. cities which have long range plans can make better use
       of the funds spent by the government during a depression
    D. long range objectives help a city to devise new plans
       for the development of parks, schools and other public
       improvements at a considerable saving

13. "Increment or decrement in city income hangs largely upon   13.____
    the maintenance of the values and valuations of real property,
    upon the quantity of new improvements that go into the city,
    upon the profitableness of real estate, upon the advent of
    booms and depressions, and upon the flow of people into or out
    of the city."
    According to the preceding statement,
    A. a boom or a depression has a marked effect on the flow
       of people into or out of a city
    B. new improvements that go into a city enhance the profitable-
       ness of real estate
    C. real estate values, which form the major basis of a city's
       taxation, are the sources of city salaries
    D. the variation of a city's income depends on the values of
       the real estate in the city

14. "The institution of the family is a vitally important part 14.____
    of all human societies, but in modern society, particularly,
    various organized services have developed that enable some
    people to secure some of the most essential benefits of
    family life without belonging to a family group."
    Of the following, the LEAST valid inference on the basis of
    the preceding statement is that
    A. people who are not part of a family unit can obtain most
       of the essential benefits of family life by contacting
       an appropriate social agency
    B. present day society offers an opportunity to some who
       are not members of a family unit to share in some of the
       benefits of family living
    C. the institution of the family is not native to modern
       society alone
    D. to obtain the benefits of family life it is usually
       necessary to belong to a family group

15. "Reform organizations seek, as a rule, to bring about a   15.____
    specific economic or political change; social work agencies
    are usually occupied with the task of meeting existing situa-
    tions in the lives of particular individuals or groups."
    According to the preceding statement,
    A. a reform organization is concerned with helping the
       individual by changing some factor in the environment
       which the individual feels is too arduous to accept
    B. a reform organization is not concerned with the ability
       of the individual to meet his social responsibilities
    C. social work agencies are not concerned with any specific
       economic or political change because this does not involve
       the individual's personal adjustment
    D. social workers are primarily concerned with helping their
       clients to meet current living conditions

16. "Adequate facilities for education, recreation and health 16.____
    must be provided for children, and social conditions created
    that promote the child's development into a law-abiding
    citizen. It is not the task of social work to provide
    these facilities but to direct children to them and to help
    them to use these facilities."
    Of the following, the *most accurate* statement on the basis
    of the preceding statement is that
        A. a child who does not have adequate educational, re-
           creational and health facilities will develop into a
           poor citizen
        B. the education of the public to the importance of pro-
           viding adequate facilities for children is primarily
           the social worker's responsibility
        C. the proper use of leisure time by children is an im-
           portant aspect of the social worker's job
        D. the three most important needs of a child which must
           be satisfied first are those of education, recreation
           and health

17. "Social workers start from the assumption that preservation 17.____
    of the family as the basic unit of social living is their
    accepted objective. In view of the frequency of divorce
    and the breakdown of authority in the home, social work
    now makes articulate its concern for family integrity."
    According to the preceding statement,
        A. failure to keep the family as a basic unit leads to a
           breakdown of authority in the home, upsetting family
           integrity
        B. in extreme cases where divorce is inevitable a social
           worker must accept the breakdown of the family unit
        C. social workers are primarily concerned with keeping
           a family together as a basic entity of social living
        D. the importance of the family to society has been demon-
           strated by experience with children who have been
           institutionalized

18. "The marked change in the spirit in which social work is 18.____
    carried on is evidenced in the adoption of business methods
    of organization, including centralized purchasing of supplies
    for social agencies, cost accounting, careful budgeting and
    auditing of accounts, evaluation of methods and publication
    of reports. Trained personnel for defined jobs is increasingly
    sought, and there is appreciation of the differentiated abilities
    required in the social agency."
    According to the preceding statement,
        A. it is apparent that the adoption of business methods of
           organization has resulted in a chage in the method of
           preparing case work reports
        B. social work agencies that train people for definite jobs
           achieve savings in social work that approximate those of
           business organization.
        C. social work now uses current business procedures in
           carrying forward the pruposes of a social agency
        D. trained personnel in social work are responsible for
           the adoption of business methods of procedure

19. "Basic to the functioning of the professional social   19.____
    worker is an understanding of human personality and of
    the world we live in."
    The one of the following which is the *most accurate*
    statement on the basis of the preceding quotation is that
    A. a social worker must be familiar with human behavior
       in order to be able to perform his work properly
    B. a social worker who understands human personality
       is able to function better as a citizen of the world
    C. social work may be classified as a profession because,
       for its proper performance, a basic understanding of the
       social and biological sciences is required
    D. through his daily contact with his clients a social
       worker will obtain a better understanding of the world
       he lives in

QUESTIONS 20-24.
Questions 20-24 each consist of three words. For each item, select
the word which is INCORRECTLY spelled and write the capital letter
preceding that work in the correspondingly numbered space on your
answer sheet.

20. A. achievment   B. maintenance   20.____
    C. questionnaire   D. all are correct

21. A. prevelant   B. pronunciation   21.____
    C. separate   D. all are correct

22. A. permissible   B. relevant   22.____
    C. seize   D. all are correct

23. A. corroborate   B. desparate   23.____
    C. eighth   D. all are correct

24. A. exceed   B. feasibility   24.____
    C. psycological   D. all are correct

QUESTIONS 25-29.
Use the material which follows in answering questions 25-29.
Copy I on the following page is an accurate copy of material which is
to be prepared for the printer. Copy II of this material contains a
number of typographical errors. Compare Copy II with Copy I and find
the typographical errors. Every group of five lines in Copy II is
numbered. Indicate the number of typographical errors in each group
of five lines of Copy II by writing in the correspondingly numbered
space on the answer sheet the capital letter preceding the best of
the following alternatives:

    A. no errors   B. 1-2 errors
    C. 3-4 errors   D. 5 or more errors

COPY I

Parcel 1. Beginning at a point formed by the intersection of the northerly side of 73rd avenue with the westerly side of Francis Lewis boulevard as said streets are indicated upon the final map of the borough of Queens known as Alteration Map No. 2831 adopted by the board of estimate on May 15, 1941; running thence northerly along the westerly side of Francis Lewis boulevard following a curve having a radius of 8,053 feet for a distance of 585.15 feet; thence northerly along the westerly side of Francis Lewis boulevard in a straight line for a distance of 687.43 feet; thence northerly along the westerly side of Francis Lewis boulevard and its prolongation following a curve having a radius of 5,677 feet for a distance of 509.79 feet to the old southerly side of North Hempstead turnpike as formerly laid out and as shown discontinued upon the aforementioned final city map; thence easterly along said southerly side of North Hempstead turnpike for 110.12 feet to the easterly side of Francis Lewis boulevard; thence southerly along the easterly side of Francis Lewis boulevard following a curve having a radius of 5.783 feet for a distance of 489.20 feet; thence southerly along the easterly side of Francis Lewis boulevard in a straight line for a distance of 687.43 feet; thence southerly along the easterly side of Francis Lewis boulevard following a curve having a radius of 7,947 feet for a distance of 572.90 feet to the northerly side of 73rd avenue.

COPY II

25. Parcel 1: Beginning at point formed by the intersection   25.____
    of the northerly side of 73d Avenue with the westerly side of
    Francis Lewis boulevard as said streets are indicated upon the
    final map of the borough of Queens known as Alteration Map
    No. 2831 adapted by the board of estimate on May 15, 1941;

26. running thence northerly along the westerly side of Francis   26.____
    Lewis boulevard following a curve having a radius of 8,053
    feet for a distance of 585.15 feet; thence northerly along the
    westerly side of Francis Lewis boulevard in a straight line for
    a distance of 687.43 feet; thence northerly along

27. the westerly side of Francis Lewis boulevard and its   27.____
    prolongation following a curve having a radius of 5.677
    feet for a distance of 509.79 feet to the old southerly side
    of North Hempstead Turnpike as formerly laid out and is
    shown discontinued upon the aforementioned final city map;
    thence easterly

28. along said southerly side of North Hempstead turnpike   28.____
    for 1101.2 feet to the easterly side of Francis Lewsis
    boulevard; thence southerly along the easterly side of Francis
    Lewis boulevard following a curve having a radius of 5.783
    feet for a distance of 489.20 feet; thence southerly along
    the easterly

29. side of Francis Lewis boulevard in a straight line for   29.____
    a distance of 687.43 feet; thence southerly along the
    easterly side of Francis Lewis boulevard following a curve
    having a radius of 7,947 feet for a distance of 572.90 feet
    to the northerly side of 73d avenue.

30. "He described a hypothetical situation to illustrate his   30.____
    point." In the preceding sentence, the word "hypothetical"
    means *most nearly*
        A. actual   B. theoretical
        C. typical   D. unusual

31. "I gave tacit approval to my partner's proposed business   31.____
    changes." In the preceding sentence, the word "tacit"
    means *most nearly*
        A. enthusiastic   B. partial
        C. silent   D. written

32. "Jones was considered an "astute lawyer by the members   32.____
    of his profession." In the preceding sentence, the word
    "astute" means *most nearly*
        A. clever   B. persevering
        C. poorly trained   D. unethical

33. "There were intimations even in early days of the way in   33.____
    which he would go." In the preceding sentence, the word
    "intimations" means *most nearly*
        A. hints   B. patterns
        C. plans   D. purposes

34. "His last book was published posthumously." In the pre-   34.____
    ceding sentence, the word "posthumously" means *most nearly*
        A. after the death of the author
        B. printed free by the publisher
        C. without a dedication
        D. without royalties

35. "When he was challenged, he used every known subterfuge."   35.____
    In the preceding sentence, the word "subterfuge" means
    most nearly
        A. evasion to justify one's conduct
        B. means of attack to defend one's self
        C. medical device
        D. unconscious thought

36. "His partner suggested a course of action that would   36.____
    alleviate the difficulties which confronted him." In the
    preceding sentence, the word "alleviate" means *most nearly*
        A. correct   B. lessen
        C. remove   D. solve

37. "Among the applicants for the new apartment white collar   37.____
    workers were preponderant." In the preceding sentence,
    the word "preponderant" means *most nearly*
        A. considered not eligible   B. in evidence
        C. superior in number   D. the first to apply

38. "The captain gave a lucid explanation of his plans for the 38.____
    coming campaign." In the preceding sentence, the word
    "lucid" means *most nearly*
    A. clear   B. graphic
    C. interesting   D. thorough

39. "He led a sedentary life." In the preceding sentence, the 39.____
    word "sedentary" means *most nearly*
    A. aimless   B. exciting
    C. full   D. inactive

40. "His plan for the next campaign was very plausible." In the 40.____
    preceding sentence, the word "plausible" means *most nearly*
    A. appropriate   B. believable
    C. usable   D. valuable

KEY (CORRECT ANSWERS)

1. D	11. D	21. A	31. C
2. A	12. C	22. D	32. A
3. C	13. D	23. B	33. A
4. A	14. A	24. C	34. A
5. D	15. D	25. C	35. A
6. B	16. C	26. A	36. B
7. B	17. C	27. C	37. C
8. C	18. C	28. B	38. A
9. D	19. A	29. B	39. D
10. D	20. A	30. B	40. B

EXAMINATION SECTION

DIRECTIONS: Each question or incomplete statement is followed by
several suggested answers or completions. Select the
one that BEST answers the question or completes the
statement. *PRINT THE LETTER OF THE CORRECT ANSWER IN
THE SPACE AT THE RIGHT.*

1. Of the following, the most recent amendment to the Consti-   1._____
   tution of the United States is concerned with the
   A. appointment of electors for President and Vice-President
      by the District of Columbia
   B. commencement of term of office of President, Vice-President
      and members of Congress
   C. election of Senators
   D. number of terms of office any person may serve as President
      of the United States

2. The Federal system of "checks and balances" is based   2._____
   upon the principle that:
   A. All powers not delegated by the Constitution to the
      Federal government are reserved to the states and the
      subdivisions thereof
   B. Although the two major political parties usually share
      the responsibility of conducting governmental affairs,
      minor parties may be mandated by the people to do so
      when the occasion arises
   C. A republic is a form of government in which people rule
      themselves by freely electing representatives and a chief
      executive, who can be impeached, if necessary
   D. By not giving any branch of our national government com-
      plete power, the people prevent any one branch from be-
      coming too powerful

3. The agency responsible for the national influenza immuniza- 3._____
   tion program is the
   A. Federal Food and Drug Administration
   B. Federal Welfare Administration
   C. United States Division of Quarantine
   D. United States Public Health Service

4. The United States' balance of international payments mea-   4._____
   sures the nation's transactions with foreign countries. The
   Federal agency which is responsible for the analysis of data
   in this regard is the
   A. Federal Trade Commission
   B. Interstate Commerce Commission
   C. U.S. Department of Commerce
   D. U.S. Tariff Commission

5. Of the following, the *most important* reason for the constitutional provision that all bills for raising revenue be introduced first in the House of Representatives is that
    A. both houses have the power to levy and collect taxes, and to pay the just debts of the United States government
    B. Senators hold office for six years while members of the House of Representatives hold office for only two years
    C. the House of Representatives, by composition, is more directly representative of all the people of the country
    D. the Senate has the right to amend such bills if it does not agree with their provisions

5. ___

6. The unemployment rate in the United States for the past few years has been approximately
    A. 4½%   B. 7%   C. 9½%   D. 12%

6. ___

7. Of the following, the one indicating the correct order of succession to the Presidency of the United States in the event of the death of the current President is the
    A. Vice-President, Secretary of State, the President pro tempore of the Senate, the Secretary of Defense, and the Secretary of the Treasury
    B. Vice-President, Secretary of State, the Speaker of the House of Representatives, the President pro tempore of the Senate, the Secretary of the Treasury
    C. Vice-President, Speaker of the House of Representatives, the President pro tempore of the Senate, the Secretary of State, the Secretary of the Treasury
    D. Vice-President, Speaker of the House of Representatives, the Secretary of State, the President pro tempore of the Senate, the Secretary of Defense

7. ___

8. The highest court in New York State is the
    A. Apellate Division of the Supreme Court
    B. Court of Appeals
    C. Court of Claims
    D. Supreme Court

8. ___

9. The state banking department supervises thousands of licensed institutions with many $billions in assets. From time to time, without warning, department examiners visit these institutions.
    Of the following, the *principal* reason for this action is to
    A. catch embezzlers
    B. collect proper assessments
    C. investigate the qualifications of bank personnel
    D. provide a basis for changes in bank management procedures

9. ___

10. More than a third of the state's annual budget goes to the Education Department. The responsibility for the proper expenditures of these funds is vested basically in the
    A. Board of Governors of the State University
    B. Board of Regents of the University of the State
    C. Board of Trustees of the State Education Department
    D. State Education Commissioner

10. ___

11. The Department of State has a wide variety of governmental 11.____
functions. It
   A. audits all claims against the state before payment
   B. classifies positions in state service according to
      duties and salary
   C. has jurisdiction over the policies   and rates of all
      forms of insurance
   D. regulates the operation of bingo games

12. The countries which have comprised the Central Treaty   12.____
Organization are:
   A. Egypt, Jordan, Syria and Pakistan
   B. Great Britain, Iran, Pakistan, and Turkey
   C. Iran, Iraq, Jordan and Syria
   D. Iran, Israel, Pakistan and Turkey

13. The Soviet Union annually celebrates the "October Rev-   13.____
olution" which took place in
   A. 1913   B. 1915   C. 1917   D. 1921

14. Of the following, the most accurate statement concerning   14.____
the Ecumenical Council which met in Rome is
   A. the Council meetings are regularly scheduled events in
      the Roman Catholic calendar
   B. the Council last met in 1870
   C. the current Council seeks to make the celebration of
      the mass acceptable to all Protestants
   D. the current Council received no cooperation from any
      Protestant sect

15. The Federal Reserve Board changes margin requirements for   15.____
stock transactions *principally* to
   A. control stock market speculation
   B. encourage investment in corporate bonds
   C. help increase the gross national product
   D. prevent an excess flow of gold from the United States
      to foreign countries

16. The Fire Next Time was on the best-seller list in the   16.____
early sixties. The book was concerned with:
   A. Advocacy of segregation
   B. A forthright protest against segregation
   C. The possible destruction of the earth due to heat
      generated by fall-out radiation if atomic weapons
      were to be used in another war
   D. The famous historical incident of the fire in the
      Triangle Shirtwaist Company in New York City and its
      consequences

17. The Wine Is Bitter was on the best-seller list and was   17.____
concerned with
   A. American aid in South America
   B. Poverty in Southern Italy
   C. The activities of the Central Intelligence Agency
   D. The use of wine in cookery

4

QUESTIONS 18-27.
For each question numbered 18 to 27 select the choice whose meaning is most nearly the same as that of the numbered item.

18. ACHROMATIC
    A. colorless
    C. timeless
    B. involuntary
    D. unmusical
                                                                18.____

19. ALTER EGO
    A. business partner
    C. guide
    B. confidential friend
    D. subconscious conflict
                                                                19.____

20. FOURTH ESTATE
    A. the aristocracy
    C. the judiciary
    B. the clergy
    D. the newspapers
                                                                20.____

21. IMPEACH
    A. accuse
    C. remove
    B. find guilty
    D. try
                                                                21.____

22. PROPENSITY
    A. dislike
    C. inclination
    B. helpfulness
    D. supervision
                                                                22.____

23. SPLENETIC
    A. charming
    C. shining
    B. peevish
    D. sluggish
                                                                23.____

24. SUBORN
    A. bribe someone to commit perjury
    B. demote someone several levels in rank
    C. deride
    D. substitute
                                                                24.____

25. TALISMAN
    A. charm
    C. prayer shawl
    B. juror
    D. native
                                                                25.____

26. VITREOUS
    A. corroding
    C. nourishing
    B. glassy
    D. sticky
                                                                26.____

27. WRY
    A. comic
    C. resilient
    B. grained
    D. twisted
                                                                27.____

QUESTIONS 28-37.

In each of the questions numbered 28 to 37, only one of the four sentences conforms to standards of correct usage. The other three contain errors in grammar, diction, punctuation or spelling. Select the choice in each question which *best* conforms to standards of correct usage.

Consider a choice correct if it contains none of the errors mentioned above, even though there may be other correct ways of expressing the same thought.

28. A. Although we understood that for him music was a passion, 28.____
       we were disturbed by the fact that he was addicted to
       sing along with the soloists.
    B. Do you believe that Steven is liable to win a scholarship?
    C. Give the picture to whomever is a connoisseur of art.
    D. Whom do you believe to be the most efficient worker in
       the office?

29. A. Each adult who is sure they know all the answers will   29.____
       some day realize their mistake.
    B. Even the most hardhearted villain would have to feel
       bad about so horrible a tragedy.
    C. Neither being licensed teachers, both aspirants had to
       pass rigorous tests before being appointed.
    D. The principal reason why he wanted to be designated was
       because he had never before been to a convention.

30. A. Being that the weather was so inclement, the party   30.____
       has been postponed for at least a month.
    B. He is in New York City only three weeks and he has
       already seen all the thrilling sights in Manhattan
       and in the other four boroughs.
    C. If you will look it up in the official directory, which
       can be consulted in the library during specified hours,
       you will discover that the chairman and director are Mr.
       T. Henry Long.
    D. Working hard at college during the day and at the post
       office during the night, he appeared to his family to
       be indefatigable.

31. A. I would have been happy to oblige you if you only asked 31.____
       me to do it.
    B. The cold weather, as well as the unceasing wind and rain,
       have made us decide to spend the winter in Florida.
    C. The politician would have been more successful in winning
       office if he would have been less dogmatic
    D. These trousers are expensive; however, they will wear well.

32. A. All except him wore formal attire at the reception for   32.____
       the ambassador.
    B. If that chair were to be blown off of the balcony, it
       might injure someone below.
    C. Not a passenger, who was in the crash, survived the impact.
    D. To borrow money off friends is the best way to lose them.

33. A. Approaching Manhattan on the ferry boat from Staten   33.____
       Island, an unforgettable sight of the skyscrapers is seen.
    B. Did you see the exhibit of modernistic paintings as yet?
    C. Gesticulating wildly and ranting in stentorian tones, the
       speaker was the sinecure of all eyes.
    D. The airplane with crew and passengers was lost somewhere in
       the Pacific Ocean.

34. A. If one has consistently had that kind of training, it   34.____
       is certainly too late to change your entire method of
       swimming long distances.
    B. The captain would have been more impressed if you would
       have been more conscientious in evacuation drills.
    C. The passangers on the stricken ship were all ready to
       abandon it at the signal.
    D. The villainous shark lashed at the lifeboat with it's tail,
       trying to upset the rocking boat in order to partake of
       it's contents.

35. A. As one whose been certified as a professional engineer,   35.____
       I belive that the decision to build a bridge over that
       harbor is unsound.
    B. Between you and me, this project ought to be completed
       long before winter arrives.
    C. He fervently hoped that the men would be back at camp and
       to find them busy at their usual chores.
    D. Much to his surprise, he discovered that the climate of
       Korea was like his home town.

36. A. An industrious executive is aided, not impeded, by   36.____
       having a hobby which gives him a fresh point of view
       on life and its problems.
    B. Frequent absence during the calendar year will surely
       mitigate against the chances of promotion.
    C. He was unable to go to the comittee meeting because he
       was very ill.
    D. Mr. Brown expressed his disapproval so emphatically that
       his associates were embarassed.

37. A. At our next session, the office manager will have told   37.____
       you something about his duties and responsibilities.
    B. In general, the book is absorbing and original and have
       no hesitation about recommending it.
    C. The procedures followed by private industry in dealing
       with lateness and absence are different from ours.
    D. We shall treat confidentially any information about Mr.
       Doe, to whom we understand you have sent reports to for
       many years.

QUESTIONS 38-39.
Questions 38 and 39 are to be answered on the basis of the information contained in the passage given below.

There have been almost as many definitions of "opinion" as there have been students of the problem, and the definitions have ranged from such a statement as "inconsistent views capable of being accepted by rational minds as true, " to the "overt manifestation of an attitude."

There are, however, a number of clearly outstanding factors among various definitions which form the sum total of the concept. Opinion is the stronghold of the individual. No "group" ever had an opinion, and there is no mechanism except that of the individual mind capable of forming an opinion. It is true, of course, that opinions can be altered or even created by the stimuli of environment. In the midst of individual diversity and confusion every question as it rises into importance is subjected to a process of consolidation and clarification until there emerge certain views, each held and advocated in common by bodies of citizens. When a group of people accept the same opinion, that opinion is public with respect to the group accepting it. When there is not unanimous opinion, there is not one public but two or more.

38. On the basis of the above passage, it may be inferred that: 38.____
    A. All individual opinions are subjected to consolidation by the influence of environmental stimuli
    B. Government is influenced by opinions held in common by large groups of citizens
    C. Some of the elements of the extremely varied definitions of "opinion" are compatible
    D. When there is no unanimity, there is no public opinion

39. On the basis of the above passage, the *most accurate* of   39.____
    the following statements is:
    A. One definition of "opinion" implies that most individuals can accept inconsistent views on the same question
    B. One other definition of "opinion" implies that the individual's attitude concerning a question must be openly expressed before it can be considered as an opinion
    C. The individual opinion plays no part in the stand taken on a given question by a group after the individual has identified himself with the group
    D. There are no group opinions formed on relatively unimportant issues because of individual confusion

QUESTIONS 40-42.
Questions 40-42 are to be answered on the basis of the information contained in the passage given below.

The word "propaganda" has fallen on evil days. As far as popular usage is concerned, its reputation by now is probably lost irretrievably, for its connotation is almost invariably sinister or evil. This is a pity, for in the struggle for men's minds, it is a weapon of great potential value. Indeed, in the race against time that we are running, its constructive use is indispensible. The student of propaganda must know that it is a term honorable in origin.

"Propaganda" is "good" or "bad" according to the virtue of the end to which it seeks to persuade us, and the methods it employs. Bad propaganda is distinguished by a disregard for the welfare of those at whom it is directed. Such disregard either derives from, or eventually results in, a lack of proper reverence for individuality, for the private person and our relation to him. For "man" is substituted for "mass" and the mass is manipulated for selfish purposes. The authoritarian reformist who believes he is acting "in the interest" of the masses is also involved in this same disregard for personal integrity. Its final outcome is always the same - a disregard for the individual. Good propaganda involves the deliberate avoidance of all casuistry. In so far as good propaganda operates upon us at a level of our weakness or disability, its intent must be to contribute a cure, not a sedative; inspiration, not an opiate; enlightenment, not accentuation of our ignorance.

40. Of the following, the most suitable title for the above   40. ____
    passage is:
    A. Propaganda and Society
    B. Propaganda for the Masses
    C. The Proper Meaning of Propaganda
    D. Uses and Misuses of Propaganda

41. On the basis of the above passage, it may be inferred that 41. ____
    A. some propaganda may employ unscrupulous methods to
       persuade us to ends that are justified
    B. the definition of the word "propaganda" has been changed
    C. the method of frequent repetition is an example of bad
       propaganda
    D. the opportunity for the individual to challenge propaganda
       has decreased

42. On the basis of the above passage, it may be inferred that 42. ____
    A. a reformer who believes in his cause should not employ
       propaganda to advance it
    B. good propaganda should be limited to operating against
       the levels of weakness of the individual
    C. propaganda may lose sight of the welfare of the indivi-
       dual in its appeal to the masses
    D. those who have privileged access to the media of mass
       communication must always accept high standards in their
       use of propaganda

QUESTIONS 43-45.
Questions 43-45 are to be answered on the basis of the information
contained in the passage given below.

The context of all education is twofold - individual and social.
Its business is to make us more and more ourselves, to cultivate in
each of us our own distinctive genius, however modest it may be,
while showing us how this genius may be reconciled with the needs
and claims of the society of which we are a part. Though it is not
education's aim to cultivate eccentrics, that society is richest,
most flexible, and most humane that best uses and most tolerates
eccentricity. Conformity beyond a point breeds sterile minds and,
therefore, a sterile society.
The function of secondary - and still more of higher education-
is to affect the environment. Teachers are not, and should not be,
social reformers. But they should be the catalytic agents by means
of which young minds are influenced to desire and execute reform.
To aspire to better things is a logical and desirable part of mental
and spiritual growth.

43. Of the following, the *most suitable* title for the above   43.____
    passage is:
    A. Education's Function in Creating Individual Differences
    B. The Need for Education to Acquaint Us with Our Social
       Environment
    C. The Responsibility of Education Toward the Individual
       and Society
    D. The Role of Education in Explaining the Needs of Society

44. On the basis of the above passage, it may be inferred that 44.____
    A. conformity is one of the forerunners of totalitarianism
    B. education should be designed to create at least a modest
       amount of genius in everyone
    C. tolerance of individual differences tends to give society
       opportunities for improvement
    D. reforms are usually initiated by people who are somewhat
       eccentric

45. On the basis of the above passage, it may be inferred that 45.____
    A. genius is likely to be accompanied by a desire for
       social reform
    B. nonconformity is an indication of the inquiring mind
    C. people who are not high school or college graudates are not
       able to affect the environment
    D. teachers may or may not be social reformers

QUESTIONS 46-47.
Questions 46-47 are to be answered on the basis of the information contained in the passage given below.

If you like people, if you seek contact with them rather than hide yourself in a corner, if you study your fellow men sympathetically, if you try consistently to contribute something to their success and happiness, if you are reasonably generous with your thoughts and your time, if you have a partial reserve with everyone but a seeming reserve with no one, you will get along with your superiors, your subordinates, and the human race.

By the scores of thousands, precepts and platitudes have been written for the guidance of personal conduct. The odd part of it is that, despite all of this labor, most of the frictions in modern society arise from the individual's feeling of inferiority, his false pride, his vanity, his unwillingness to yield space to any other man and his consequent urge to throw his own weight around. Goethe said that the quality which best enables a man to renew his own life, in his relation to others, is his capability of renouncing particular things at the right moment in order warmly to embrace something new in the next.

46. On the basis of the above passage, it may be inferred that 46._____
    A. a person should be unwilling to renounce privileges
    B. a person should realize that loss of a desirable job assignment may come at an opportune moment
    C. it is advisable for a person to maintain a considerable amount of reserve in his relationship with unfamiliar people
    D. people should be ready to contribute generously to a worthy charity

47. Of the following, the *most valid* implication made by the   47._____
    above passage is that
    A. a wealthy person who spends a considerable amount of money entertaining his friends is not really getting along with them
    B. if a person studies his fellow men carefully and impartially, he will tend to have good relationships with them
    C. individuals who maintain seemingly little reserve in their relationships with people have in some measure overcome their own feelings of inferiority
    D. most precepts that have been written for the guidance of personal conduct in relationships with other people have been invalid

48. Of the following, the *most accurate* statement concerning   48._____
    public television is
    A. it is financed solely by funds solicited from the public
    B. it is supported by a combination of private and public grants and funds solicited from the general public
    C. its programs are concerned with education and the station operates only during school hours.
    D. its programs are mainly educational and cultural, but some are commercial

49. Graduates of the two-year courses offered by the various   49.____
    community colleges receive degrees of:
      A. Associate in Arts, or Applied Science
      B. Graduate in Arts, or Applied Science
      C. Certificant in Arts, or Applied Science
      D. Pre-Bachelor of Arts, or Applied Science

50. John Steinbeck, the Nobel Prize winner, authored the book   50.____
    "Travels with Charlie". "Charlie" is the name
      A. he gave to the trailer he used in his travels
      B. he uses familiarly to his wife
      C. of a fictional character in the book
      D. of his dog

KEY (CORRECT ANSWERS)

1. A	11. D	21. A	31. D	41. A
2. D	12. B	22. C	32. A	42. C
3. D	13. C	23. B	33. D	43. C
4. C	14. B	24. A	34. C	44. C
5. C	15. A	25. A	35. B	45. D
6. C	16. B	26. B	36. A	46. B
7. C	17. A	27. D	37. C	47. C
8. B	18. A	28. D	38. C	48. B
9. D	19. B	29. B	39. B	49. A
10. B	20. D	30. D	40. D	50. D

EXAMINATION SECTION

DIRECTIONS: Each question or incomplete statement is followed by
several suggested answers or completions. Select the
one that BEST answers the question or completes the
statement. *PRINT THE LETTER OF THE CORRECT ANSWER IN
THE SPACE AT THE RIGHT.*

1. Good procedure in handling complaints from the public may   1.___
    be divided into the following four principal stages:
       I. Investigation of the complaint
      II. Receipt of the complaint
     III. Assignment of responsibility for investigation and
          correction
      IV. Notification of correction

    The ORDER in which these stages ordinarily come is:
       A. III, II, I, IV   B. II, III, I, IV
       C. II, III, IV, I   D. II, IV, III, I

2. The department may expect the MOST severe public   2.___
    criticism if
       A. it asks for an increase in its annual budget
       B. it purchases new and costly street cleaning equipment
       C. sanitation officers and men are reclassified to higher
          salary grades
       D. there is delay in cleaning streets of snow

3. The MOST important function of public relations in the   3.___
    department should be to
       A. develop cooperation on the part of the public in
          keeping streets clean
       B. get stricter penalties enacted for health code
          violations
       C. recruit candidates for entrance positions who can
          be developed into supervisors
       D. train career personnel so that they can advance in
          the department

4. The one of the following which has MOST frequently   4.___
    elicited unfavorable public comment has been
       A. dirty sidewalks or streets
       B. dumping on lots
       C. failure to curb dogs
       D. overflowing garbage cans

5. It has been suggested that, as a public relations measure,   5.__
    sections hold *open house* for the public.
    The MOST effective time for this would be
       A. during the summer when children are not in school
          and can accompany their parents
       B. during the winter when snow is likely to fall and
          the public can see snow removal preparations

    C. immediately after a heavy snow storm when department
       snow removal operations are in full progress
    D. when street sanitation is receiving general attention
       as during *Keep City Clean* week

6. When a public agency conducts a public relations program,   6.___
it is MOST likely to find that each recipient of its
message will
    A. disagree with the basic purpose of the message if the
       officials are not well known to him
    B. accept the message if it is presented by someone
       perceived as having a definite intention to persuade
    C. ignore the message unless it is presented in a
       literate and clever manner
    D. give greater attention to certain portions of the
       message as a result of his individual and cultural
       differences

7. Following are three statements about public relations and   7.___
communications:
    I. A person who seeks to influence public opinion can
      speed up a trend
   II. Mass communications is the exposure of a mass
      audience to an idea
 III. All media are equally effective in reaching opinion
      leaders

Which of the following choices CORRECTLY classifies the
above statements into those which are correct and those
which are not?
    A. I and II are correct, but III is not
    B. II and III are correct, but I is not
    C. I and III are correct, but II is not
    D. III is correct, but I and II are not

8. Public relations experts say that MAXIMUM effect for a   8.___
message results from
    A. concentrating in one medium
    B. ignoring mass media and concentrating on *opinion makers*
    C. presenting only those factors which support a given
       position
    D. using a combination of two or more of the available
       media

9. To assure credibility and avoid hostility, the public   9.___
relations man MUST
    A. make certain his message is truthful, not evasive or
       exaggerated
    B. make sure his message contains some dire consequence
       if ignored
    C. repeat the message often enough so that it cannot be
       ignored
    D. try to reach as many people and groups as possible

10. The public relations man MUST be prepared to assume that   10.___
    members of his audience
      A. may have developed attitudes toward his proposals --
         favorable, neutral, or unfavorable
      B. will be immediately hostile
      C. will consider his proposals with an open mind
      D. will invariably need an introduction to his subject

11. The one of the following statements that is CORRECT is: 11.___
      A. When a stupid question is asked of you by the public,
         it should be disregarded
      B. If you insist on formality between you and the public,
         the public will not be able to ask stupid questions
         that cannot be answered
      C. The public should be treated courteously, regardless
         of how stupid their questions may be
      D. You should explain to the public how stupid their
         questions are

12. With regard to public relations, the MOST important item   12.___
    which should be emphasized in an employee training program
    is that
      A. each inspector is a public relations agent
      B. an inspector should give the public all the information
         it asks for
      C. it is better to make mistakes and give erroneous infor-
         mation than to tell the public that you do not know the
         correct answer to their problem
      D. public relations is so specialized a field that only
         persons specially trained in it should consider it

13. Members of the public frequently ask about departmental   13.___
    procedures.
    Of the following, it is BEST to
      A. advise the public to put the question in writing so
         that he can get a proper formal reply
      B. refuse to answer because this is a confidential matter
      C. explain the procedure as briefly as possible
      D. attempt to avoid the issue by discussing other matters

14. The effectiveness of a public relations program in a   14.___
    public agency such as the authority is BEST indicated by
    the
      A. amount of mass media publicity favorable to the
         policies of the authority
      B. morale of those employees who directly serve the
         patrons of the authority
      C. public's understanding and support of the authority's
         program and policies
      D. number of complaints received by the authority from
         patrons using its facilities

15. In an attempt to improve public opinion about a certain   15.___
    idea, the BEST course of action for an agency to take
    would be to present the
      A. clearest statements of the idea even though the
         language is somewhat technical

B. idea as the result of long-term studies
C. idea in association with something familiar to most people
D. idea as the viewpoint of the majority leaders

16. The fundamental factor in any agency's community relations program is
    A. an outline of the objectives
    B. relations with the media
    C. the everyday actions of the employees
    D. a well-planned supervisory program

16.___

17. The FUNDAMENTAL factor in the success of a community relations program is
    A. true commitment by the community
    B. true commitment by the administration
    C. a well-planned, systematic approach
    D. the actions of individuals in their contacts with the public

17.___

18. The statement below which is LEAST correct is:
    A. Because of selection standards, the supervisor frequently encounters problems resulting from subordinates' inability to express themselves in the language of the profession
    B. Distortion of the meaning of a communication is usually brought about by a failure to use language that has a precise meaning to others
    C. The term *filtering* is the distortion or dilution of content of a communication that occurs as information is passed from individual to individual
    D. The complexity of the *communications net* will directly affect the speed and accuracy of messages flowing through it

18.___

19. Consider the following three statements that may or may not be CORRECT:
    I. In order to prevent the stifling of communications flow, supervisors should insist that employees use the formal communications network
    II. Two-way communications are faster and more accurate than one-way communications
    III. There is a direct correlation between the effectiveness of communications and the total setting in which they occur

    The choice below which MOST accurately describes the above statement is:
    A. All 3 are correct
    B. All 3 are incorrect
    C. More than one of the statements is correct
    D. Only one of the statements is correct

19.___

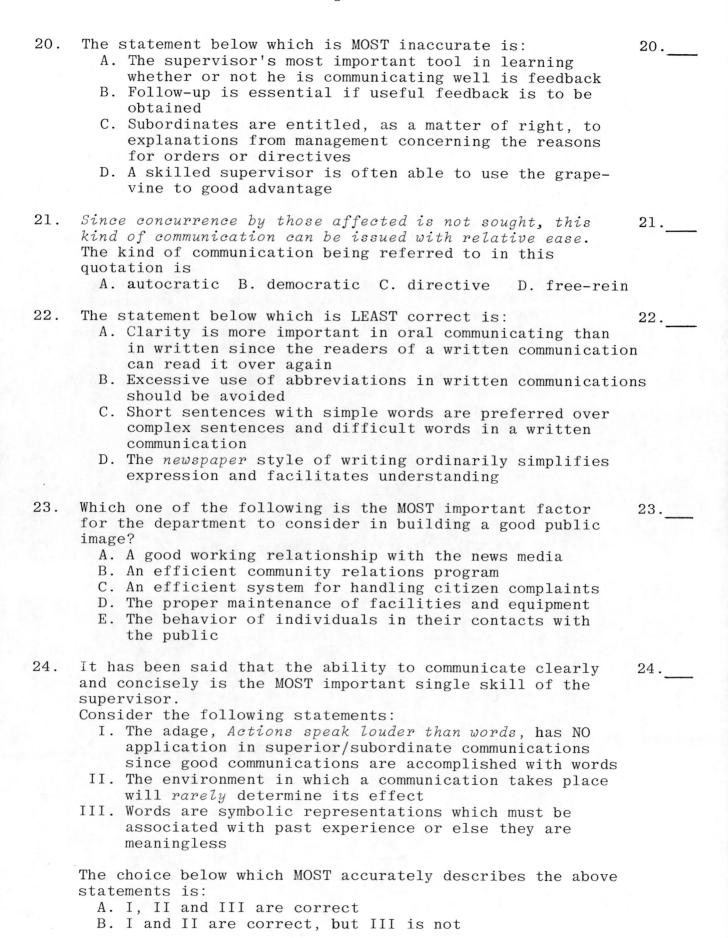

20. The statement below which is MOST inaccurate is:
    A. The supervisor's most important tool in learning
       whether or not he is communicating well is feedback
    B. Follow-up is essential if useful feedback is to be
       obtained
    C. Subordinates are entitled, as a matter of right, to
       explanations from management concerning the reasons
       for orders or directives
    D. A skilled supervisor is often able to use the grape-
       vine to good advantage

    20.____

21. *Since concurrence by those affected is not sought, this
kind of communication can be issued with relative ease.*
The kind of communication being referred to in this
quotation is
    A. autocratic B. democratic C. directive D. free-rein

    21.____

22. The statement below which is LEAST correct is:
    A. Clarity is more important in oral communicating than
       in written since the readers of a written communication
       can read it over again
    B. Excessive use of abbreviations in written communications
       should be avoided
    C. Short sentences with simple words are preferred over
       complex sentences and difficult words in a written
       communication
    D. The *newspaper* style of writing ordinarily simplifies
       expression and facilitates understanding

    22.____

23. Which one of the following is the MOST important factor
for the department to consider in building a good public
image?
    A. A good working relationship with the news media
    B. An efficient community relations program
    C. An efficient system for handling citizen complaints
    D. The proper maintenance of facilities and equipment
    E. The behavior of individuals in their contacts with
       the public

    23.____

24. It has been said that the ability to communicate clearly
and concisely is the MOST important single skill of the
supervisor.
Consider the following statements:
    I. The adage, *Actions speak louder than words*, has NO
      application in superior/subordinate communications
      since good communications are accomplished with words
   II. The environment in which a communication takes place
      will *rarely* determine its effect
 III. Words are symbolic representations which must be
      associated with past experience or else they are
      meaningless

The choice below which MOST accurately describes the above
statements is:
    A. I, II and III are correct
    B. I and II are correct, but III is not

    24.____

C. I and III are correct, but II is not
D. III is correct, but I and II are not
E. I, II, and III are incorrect

25. According to expert opinion, the effectiveness of an
organization is very dependent upon good upward, downward,
and lateral communications. Lateral communications are
most important to the activity of coordinating the efforts
of organizational units. Before real communication can
take place at any level, barriers to communication must be
recognized, understood, and removed.
Consider the following three statements:
   I. The *principal* barrier to good communications is a
   failure to establish empathy between sender and
   receiver
  II. The difference in status or rank between the sender
   and receiver of a communication may be a communications barrier
 III. Communications are easier if they travel upward from
   subordinate to superior

The choice below which MOST accurately describes the above
statements is:
   A. I, II and III are incorrect
   B. I and II are incorrect
   C. I, II, and III are correct
   D. I and II are correct
   E. I and III are incorrect

25.____

KEY (CORRECT ANSWERS)

1. B	11. C
2. D	12. A
3. A	13. C
4. A	14. C
5. D	15. C
6. D	16. C
7. A	17. D
8. D	18. A
9. A	19. D
10. A	20. C

21. A
22. A
23. E
24. D
25. E

EXAMINATION SECTION
TEST 1

DIRECTIONS: Each question or incomplete statement is followed by several suggested answers or completions. Select the one that BEST answers the question or completes the statement. *PRINT THE LETTER OF THE CORRECT ANSWER IN THE SPACE AT THE RIGHT.*

1. Each of the following is one of the first considerations   1.___
   public relations practitioners should make when selecting
   the appropriate medium for message distribution EXCEPT
   A. target audience
   B. date at which audience needs to be reached
   C. possible combinations of media
   D. costs

2. Which phase of the diffusion cycle of persuasive informa-   2.___
   tion would occur LAST?
   A. Evaluation   B. Trial
   C. Awareness   D. Adoption

3. Which of the following is NOT considered to be one of the   3.___
   important psychological dimensions of public opinion?
   A. Intensity B. Duration   C. Direction D. Breadth

4. The _____ persuasion model is specifically designed to   4.___
   study the fact that an effective message is a message
   that causes a desired behavior from a person.
   A. symbolic interactionism
   B. structural functionalism
   C. sociocultural paradigm
   D. psychodynamic

5. The tryout of a public relations message on a small   5.___
   audience before general distribution is referred to as a
   A. release   B. pilot   C. hype   D. plant

6. Which of the following is NOT a title name typically held   6.___
   by government public relations practitioners?
   A. Public information officer
   B. Press secretary
   C. Director of public affairs
   D. Public relations representative

7. Which persuasive strategy involves creating a need or   7.___
   stimulating a desire?
   A. Cognitive   B. Social appeal
   C. Stimulus-response   D. Motivational

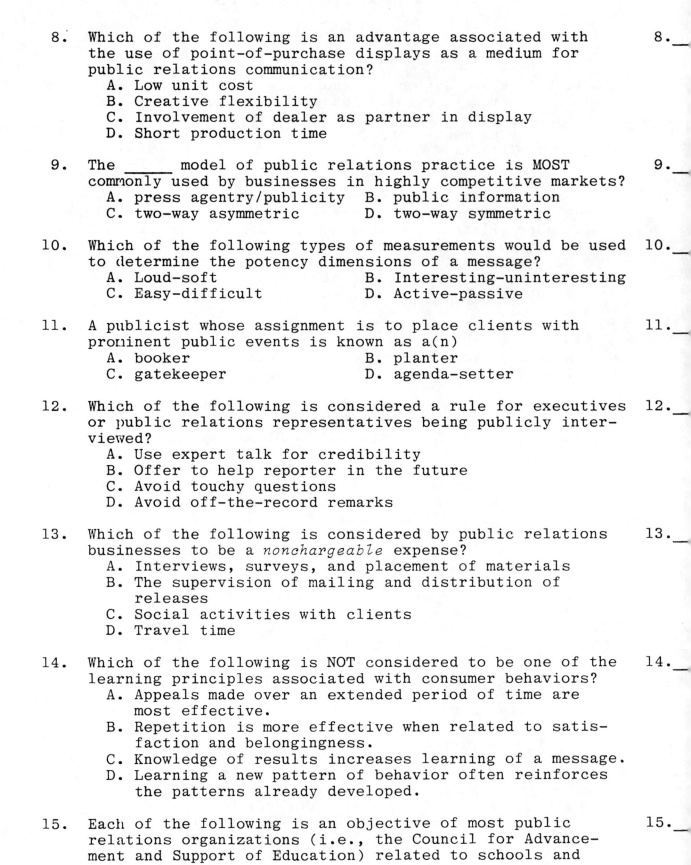

8. Which of the following is an advantage associated with   8.___
   the use of point-of-purchase displays as a medium for
   public relations communication?
   A. Low unit cost
   B. Creative flexibility
   C. Involvement of dealer as partner in display
   D. Short production time

9. The _____ model of public relations practice is MOST   9.___
   commonly used by businesses in highly competitive markets?
   A. press agentry/publicity   B. public information
   C. two-way asymmetric   D. two-way symmetric

10. Which of the following types of measurements would be used   10.___
    to determine the potency dimensions of a message?
    A. Loud-soft   B. Interesting-uninteresting
    C. Easy-difficult   D. Active-passive

11. A publicist whose assignment is to place clients with   11.___
    prominent public events is known as a(n)
    A. booker   B. planter
    C. gatekeeper   D. agenda-setter

12. Which of the following is considered a rule for executives   12.___
    or public relations representatives being publicly inter-
    viewed?
    A. Use expert talk for credibility
    B. Offer to help reporter in the future
    C. Avoid touchy questions
    D. Avoid off-the-record remarks

13. Which of the following is considered by public relations   13.___
    businesses to be a *nonchargeable* expense?
    A. Interviews, surveys, and placement of materials
    B. The supervision of mailing and distribution of
       releases
    C. Social activities with clients
    D. Travel time

14. Which of the following is NOT considered to be one of the   14.___
    learning principles associated with consumer behaviors?
    A. Appeals made over an extended period of time are
       most effective.
    B. Repetition is more effective when related to satis-
       faction and belongingness.
    C. Knowledge of results increases learning of a message.
    D. Learning a new pattern of behavior often reinforces
       the patterns already developed.

15. Each of the following is an objective of most public   15.___
    relations organizations (i.e., the Council for Advance-
    ment and Support of Education) related to schools and
    colleges EXCEPT

A. developing gift and expenditure standards
B. direct recruitment for athletics and other extra-
   curricular programs
C. improving the communication of university research
   to the public
D. helping minority leaders at institutions to advance
   their careers

16. _____ is considered a propaganda technique.   16.___
    A. Social validation   B. Transfer
    C. Suggestion of action   D. Clarification

17. Of the steps in a problem-oriented public relations cam-   17.___
    paign listed below, which would occur LAST?
    A. Determine communications strategy
    B. Evaluation of problem's impact
    C. Development of organizational strategy
    D. Deciding upon tactics

18. An organization's image is conveyed to the public and   18.___
    evaluated in each of the following areas EXCEPT
    A. financial responsibility
    B. ability to form public policy
    C. ethics
    D. social responsibility

19. Which of the following statements does NOT reflect a   19.___
    public relations principle used to help organizations to
    maintain favorable public opinion?
    A. The economic and social stability of an organization
       is dependent upon the attitudes of the public within
       its operational environment.
    B. Technology should be avoided at all costs to avoid
       distancing the organization from the public.
    C. An organization's management of communications is
       essential to its ultimate ability to adjust to
       changes necessary for longevity.
    D. All individuals have the right to information about
       pending decisions relating to them or their welfare.

20. Which communication theory claims that a society's groups 20.___
    have competing needs and interests?
    A. Evolutionary perspective
    B. Structural functionalism
    C. Sociocultural paradigm
    D. Social conflict

21. _____ is a disadvantage associated with the use of   21.___
    pamphlets and booklets as a medium for public relations
    communication.
    A. Poor color reproduction
    B. The lack of opportunity for consumer referral
    C. Difficulty in measuring effectiveness
    D. Presentation of nonspecific messages

22. In terms of psychographic research, which of the follow-   22.___
    ing personality types would be considered inner-directed?
    A. Achievers   B. Emulators
    C. Need-driven   D. Belongers

23. According to the conditional probability theory of   23.___
    message receptiveness, which type of public is the MOST
    cost-effective for message distribution?
    A(n) _____ public characterized by _____.
    A. latent; constrained behaviors
    B. active; routine behaviors
    C. active; problem-facing behaviors
    D. aware; problem-facing behaviors

24. Which of the following is NOT typically one of the   24.___
    problems associated with an organization's internal
    publications?
    A. Too much space devoted to coverage of negative issues
    B. Little attempt to show how departments inter-relate
    C. Too office-oriented
    D. Not adequately funded

25. The type of survey in which every member of the targeted   25.___
    audience has a chance of being selected for questioning
    is the _____ sample.
    A. quota   B. purposive
    C. probability   D. social

KEY (CORRECT ANSWERS)

1. C		11. A
2. D		12. B
3. B		13. C
4. D		14. D
5. B		15. B
6. D		16. B
7. D		17. D
8. B		18. B
9. C		19. B
10. A		20. D

21. C
22. C
23. D
24. A
25. C

TEST 2

DIRECTIONS: Each question or incomplete statement is followed by
                several suggested answers or completions. Select the
                one that BEST answers the question or completes the
                statement. *PRINT THE LETTER OF THE CORRECT ANSWER IN
                THE SPACE AT THE RIGHT.*

1. Increasing _____ is NOT a factor leading to the growth of   1.___
    the governmental information effort.
        A. citizen demand   B. complexity of society
        C. rural population   D. public scrutiny

2. When scheduling the preparation of public service announce-   2.___
    ments, APPROXIMATELY how much time should be set aside for
    the on-set shooting of the spot?
        A. 2-4 hours   B. 4-8 hours
        C. 8-14 hours   D. 2-3 days

3. Which of the following types of studies is used to   3.___
    measure audience attitudes before and after a public
    relations campaign?
        A. Quota sampling   B. Benchmark study
        C. Copy testing   D. Retrieval study

4. Which of the following is NOT a role of the public   4.___
    relations person during an interview?
        A. Preparer   B. Questioner
        C. Facilitator   D. Clarifier

5. A review to determine public relations material and its   5.___
    relation to the target audience is
        A. probability sampling
        B. issues management
        C. a communication audit
        D. an institutional advertisement

6. Each of the following is a guideline for publicity photo-   6.___
    graphs EXCEPT
        A. always keep the number of subjects above three
        B. keep the background neutral
        C. position subjects close together
        D. high contrast

7. The tendency of survey respondents to offer socially   7.___
    correct answers rather than ones disclosing their true
    opinions is known as
        A. courtesy bias   B. transfer
        C. encoding   D. flacking

8. Which of the following is a problem specific to the   8.___
    practice of international public relations?
        A. The containment of crises
        B. Difficulty in monitoring potentially adverse
           situations
        C. An awkwardly long chain of command
        D. Difficulty in maintaining a favorable climate for
           operations

9. Which persuasive strategy is MOST often used in an attempt   9.___
    to alleviate conditions for the poor and needy?
        A. Cognitive   B. Social appeal
        C. Stimulus-response   D. Motivational

10. The model of public relations practice MOST likely to   10.___
    involve withholding information from the public is the
    _____ model.
        A. press agentry/publicity B. public information
        C. two-way asymmetric   D. two-way symmetric

11. In relation to social services, public relations techniques 11.___
    are considered essential to each of the following practices
    EXCEPT
        A. personnel   B. client services
        C. fund-raising   D. enlistment of volunteers

12. Of the steps in scheduling an annual report listed below,   12.___
    which would occur LAST?
        A. Producing copy
        B. Assigning work
        C. Clearing material recommendations
        D. Production

13. Public relations organizations working in the United   13.___
    States for other nations can expect to perform each of
    the following tasks EXCEPT
        A. advance political objectives
        B. assist in communications in the country's own
           language
        C. counsel the country about possible United States
           reactions to activities
        D. help modify laws and regulations inhibiting client's
           activities in the United States

14. Which method for determining client charges is MOST   14.___
    commonly used by public relations practitioners?
        A. Hourly fee
        B. Fee for services and out-of-pocket expenses
        C. Fixed fee
        D. Retainer

15. What is the term for the survey technique in which   15.___
    multiple samplings drawn from the same population are
    studied longitudinally and then compared or contrasted?
       A. Census   B. Cohort study
       C. Bridge study   D. Coincidental interview

16. The communication theory which claims that social change   16.___
    follows a set of natural laws is called
       A. evolutionary perspective
       B. structural functionalism
       C. sociocultural paradigm
       D. social conflict

17. Which of the following is NOT an advantage associated   17.___
    with electronically communicated information?
       A. Exists as part of people's everyday lives
       B. Often shows events happening, as well as reports them
       C. Immediacy of message
       D. Can selectively reach desired audiences

18. Which of the following is an element of off-premise   18.___
    community relations, as practiced by the administration
    of an organization?
       A. Talks to area organizations
       B. Anniversary celebrations
       C. Corporate disclosure
       D. Tables for fundraising

19. The pursuit of management objectives through suggestions, 19.___
    recommendation, and advice is the _____ function.
       A. line   B. transfer
       C. staff   D. institutional

20. A typical public relations practitioner spends the LEAST   20.___
    amount of his/her professional time with
       A. lobbying
       B. media contacts/press conferences
       C. radio/television appearances
       D. meetings with outside groups

21. Which of the following is NOT a rule for executives or   21.___
    public relations representatives being publicly inter-
    viewed?
       A. Encourage hypothetical questions
       B. Avoid injecting yourself into the process during the
          actual interview
       C. Admit to not knowing the answer to some questions
       D. Answer questions that are public record

22. Which of the following is NOT generally considered a   22.___
    factor in determining the difficulty of an organization's
    internal communications?
       A. More sources such as television to divert workers'
          attention

    B. Increasing two-income families dilute one's interest
       in his/her job
    C. Increase in childbirth rate has produced competing
       responsibilities
    D. Increasing mobility of workers

23. The selection of a group to be polled that matches the   23.___
    characteristics of the entire audience is known as
    _____ sampling.
    A. probability   B. internal
    C. quota   D. purposive

24. The MOST important consideration in planning the compo-   24.___
    sition of an annual report is
    A. scheduling   B. photography assignments
    C. distribution   D. printing procedures

25. Which of the following is NOT an objective of government   25.___
    information efforts?
    A. Represent the public and present its interests to
       representatives
    B. Advise government management on how best to communi-
       cate a decision or program
    C. Lobby for legislation supported by public opinion
       polls
    D. Educate administrators and bureaucrats about the
       role of mass media

KEY (CORRECT ANSWERS)

1. C		11. A	
2. C		12. D	
3. B		13. B	
4. C		14. B	
5. C		15. B	
6. A		16. A	
7. A		17. D	
8. C		18. C	
9. B		19. C	
10. A		20. A	

          21. A
          22. C
          23. C
          24. A
          25. C

EXAMINATION SECTION

DIRECTIONS: Each question or incomplete statement is followed by several suggested answers or completions. Select the one that BEST answers the question or completes the statement. *PRINT THE LETTER OF THE CORRECT ANSWER IN THE SPACE AT THE RIGHT.*

1. Which of the following sentences is punctuated INCORRECTLY?   1.____
   A. Johnson said, "One tiny virus, Blanche, can multiply so fast that it will become 200 viruses in 25 minutes."
   B. With economic pressures hitting them from all sides, American farmers have become the weak link in the food chain.
   C. The degree to which this is true, of course, depends on the personalities of the people involved, the subject matter, and the atmosphere in general.
   D. "What loneliness, asked George Eliot, is more lonely than distrust?"

2. Which of the following sentences is punctuated INCORRECTLY?   2.____
   A. Based on past experiences, do you expect the plumber to show up late, not have the right parts, and overcharge you.
   B. When polled, however, the participants were most concerned that it be convenient.
   C. No one mentioned the flavor of the coffee, and no one seemed to care that china was used instead of plastic.
   D. As we said before, sometimes people view others as things; they don't see them as living, breathing beings like themselves.

3. Convention members travelled here from Kingston New York   3.____
   Pittsfield Massachusetts Bennington Vermont and Hartford Connecticut.
   How many commas should there be in the above sentence?
   A. 3   B. 4   C. 5   D. 6

4. Of the two speakers the one who spoke about human rights   4.____
   is more famous and more humble.
   How many commas should there be in the above sentence?
   A. 1   B. 2   C. 3   D. 4

5. Which sentence is punctuated INCORRECTLY?   5.____
   A. Five people voted no; two voted yes; one person abstained.
   B. Well, consider what has been said here today, but we won't make any promises.
   C. Anthropologists divide history into three major periods: the Stone Age, the Bronze Age, and the Iron Age.
   D. Therefore, we may create a stereotype about people who are unsuccessful; we may see them as lazy, unintelligent, or afraid of success.

6. Which sentence is punctuated INCORRECTLY?   6.__

    A. Studies have found that the unpredictability of
customer behavior can lead to a great deal of stress,
particularly if the behavior is unpleasant or if the
employee has little control over it.

    B. If this degree of emotion and variation can occur in
spectator sports, imagine the role that perceptions
can play when there are real stakes involved.

    C. At other times, however hidden expectations may
sabotage or severely damage an encounter without
anyone knowing what happened.

    D. There are usually four issues to look for in a
conflict: differences in values, goals, methods,
and facts.

Questions 7-10.

DIRECTIONS: Questions 7 through 10 test your ability to distinguish
between words that sound alike but are spelled differently and have different meanings. In the following
groups of sentences, one of the underlined words is
used incorrectly.

7. A. By accepting responsibility for their actions,   7.__
     managers promote trust.

    B. Dropping hints or making illusions to things that you
would like changed sometimes leads to resentment.

    C. The entire unit loses respect for the manager and
resents the reprimand.

    D. Many people are averse to confronting problems
directly; they would rather avoid them.

8. A. What does this say about the effect our expectations   8.__
     have on those we supervise?

    B. In an effort to save time between 9 A.M. and 1 P.M.,
the staff members devised their own interpretation of
what was to be done on these forms.

    C. The task master's principal concern is for getting the
work done; he or she is not concerned about the needs
or interests of employees.

    D. The advisor's main objective was increasing Angela's
ability to invest her capitol wisely.

9. A. A typical problem is that people have to cope with   9.__
     the internal censer of their feelings.

    B. Sometimes, in their attempt to sound more learned,
people speak in ways that are barely comprehensible.

    C. The council will meet next Friday to decide whether
Abrams should continue as representative.

    D. His descent from grace was assured by that final
word.

10. A. The doctor said that John's leg had to remain   10.___
        <u>stationary</u> or it would not heal properly.
    B. There is a city <u>ordinance</u> against parking too close
        to fire hydrants.
    C. Meyer's problem is that he is never <u>discrete</u> when
        talking about office politics.
    D. Mrs. Thatcher probably worked harder <u>than</u> any other
        British Prime Minister had ever worked.

Questions 11-20.

DIRECTIONS: For each of the following groups of sentences in
            Questions 11 through 20, select the sentence which
            is the BEST example of English usage and grammar.

11. A. She is a woman who, at age sixty, is distinctly   11.___
        attractive and cares about how they look.
    B. It was a seemingly impossible search, and no one
        knew the problems better than she.
    C. On the surface, they are all sweetness and light, but
        his morbid character is under it.
    D. The minicopier, designed to appeal to those who do
        business on the run like architects in the field or
        business travelers, weigh about four pounds.

12. A. Neither the administrators nor the union representa-   12.___
        tive regret the decision to settle the disagreement.
    B. The plans which are made earlier this year were no
        longer being considered.
    C. I would have rode with him if I had known he was
        leaving at five.
    D. I don't know who she said had it.

13. A. Writing at a desk, the memo was handed to her for   13.___
        immediate attention.
    B. Carla didn't water Carl's plants this week, which
        she never does.
    C. Not only are they good workers, with excellent writing
        and speaking skills, and they get to the crux of any
        problem we hand them.
    D. We've noticed that this enthusiasm for undertaking
        new projects sometimes interferes with his attention
        to detail.

14. A. It's obvious that Nick offends people by being unruly, 14.___
        inattentive, and having no patience.
    B. Marcia told Genie that she would have to leave soon.
    C. Here are the papers you need to complete your investi-
        gation.
    D. Julio was startled by you're comment.

15. A. The new manager has done good since receiving her   15.___
      promotion, but her secretary has helped her a great
      deal.
    B. One of the personnel managers approached John and
      tells him that the client arrived unexpectedly.
    C. If somebody can supply us with the correct figures,
      they should do so immediately.
    D. Like zealots, advocates seek power because they want
      to influence the policies and actions of an organiza-
      tion.

16. A. Between you and me, Chris probably won't finish this   16.___
      assignment in time.
    B. Rounding the corner, the snack bar appeared before us.
    C. Parker's radical reputation made to the Supreme Court
      his appointment impossible.
    D. By the time we arrived, Marion finishes briefing
      James and returns to Hank's office.

17. A. As we pointed out earlier, the critical determinant   17.___
      of the success of middle managers is their ability
      to communicate well with others.
    B. The lecturer stated there wasn't no reason for bad
      supervision.
    C. We are well aware whose at fault in this instance.
    D. When planning important changes, it's often wise to
      seek the participation of others because employees
      often have much valuable ideas to offer.

18. A. Joan had ought to throw out those old things that   18.___
      were damaged when the roof leaked.
    B. I spose he'll let us know what he's decided when he
      finally comes to a decision.
    C. Carmen was walking to work when she suddenly realized
      that she had left her lunch on the table as she
      passed the market.
    D. Are these enough plants for your new office?

19. A. First move the lever forward, and then they should   19.___
      lift the ribbon casing before trying to take it out.
    B. Michael finished quickest than any other person in
      the office.
    C. There is a special meeting for we committee members
      today at 4 p.m.
    D. My husband is worried about our having to work
      overtime next week.

20. A. Another source of conflicts are individuals who   20.___
      possess very poor interpersonal skills.
    B. It is difficult for us to work with him on projects
      because these kinds of people are not interested in
      team building.
    C. Each of the departments was represented at the meeting.
    D. Poor boy, he never should of past that truck on the
      right.

5

DIRECTIONS: In Questions 21 through 28, there may be a problem with English grammar or usage. If a problem does exist, select the letter that indicates the most effective change. If no problem exists, select choice A.

21. He rushed her to the hospital and stayed with her, even though this took quite a bit of his time, he didn't charge her anything.
    A. No changes are necessary
    B. Change even though to although
    C. Change the first comma to a period and capitalize even
    D. Change rushed to had rushed
    21.___

22. Waiting that appears unfairly feels longer than waiting that seems justified.
    A. No changes are necessary
    B. Change unfairly to unfair
    C. Change appears to seems
    D. Change longer to longest
    22.___

23. May be you and the person who argued with you will be able to reach an agreement.
    A. No changes are necessary
    B. Change will be to were
    C. Change argued with to had an argument with
    D. Change may be to maybe
    23.___

24. Any one of them could of taken the file while you were having coffee.
    A. No changes are necessary
    B. Change any one to anyone
    C. Change of to have
    D. Change were having to were out having
    24.___

25. While people get jobs or move from poverty level to better paying employment, they stop receiving benefits and start paying taxes.
    A. No changes are necessary
    B. Change While to As
    C. Change stop to will stop
    D. Change get to obtain
    25.___

26. Maribeth's phone rang while talking to George about the possibility of their meeting Tom at three this afternoon.
    A. No changes are necessary
    B. Change their to her
    C. Move to George so that it follows Tom
    D. Change talking to she was talking
    26.___

27. According to their father, Lisa is smarter than Chris,   27.__
    but Emily is the smartest of the three sisters.
    A. No changes are necessary
    B. Change their to her
    C. Change is to was
    D. Make two sentences, changing the second comma to a
       period and omitting but

28. Yesterday, Mark and he claim that Carl took Carol's   28.__
    ideas and used them inappropriately.
    A. No changes are necessary
    B. Change claim to claimed
    C. Change inappropriately to inappropriate
    D. Change Carol's to Carols'

Questions 29-34.

DIRECTIONS: For each group of sentences in Questions 29 through
              34, select the choice that represents the BEST editing
              of the problem sentence.

29. The managers expected employees to be at their desks at   29.__
    all times, but they would always be late or leave
    unannounced.
    A. The managers wanted employees to always be at their
       desks, but they would always be late or leave
       unannounced.
    B. Although the managers expected employees to be at
       their desks no matter what came up, they would
       always be late and leave without telling anyone.
    C. Although the managers expected employees to be at
       their desks at all times, the managers would always
       be late or leave without telling anyone.
    D. The managers expected the employee to never leave
       their desks, but they would always be late or leave
       without telling anyone.

30. The one who is department manager he will call you to   30.__
    discuss the problem tomorrow morning at 10 A.M.
    A. The one who is department manager will call you
       tomorrow morning at ten to discuss the problem.
    B. The department manager will call you to discuss the
       problem tomorrow at 10 A.M.
    C. Tomorrow morning at 10 A.M., the department manager
       will call you to discuss the problem.
    D. Tomorrow morning the department manager will call
       you to discuss the problem.

31. A conference on child care in the workplace the $200   31.__
    cost of which to attend may be prohibitive to childcare
    workers who earn less than that weekly.
    A. A conference on child care in the workplace that
       costs $200 may be too expensive for childcare
       workers who earn less than that each week.

B. A conference on child care in the workplace, the cost of which to attend is $200, may be prohibitive to childcare workers who earn less than that weekly.
C. A conference on child care in the workplace who costs $200 may be too expensive for childcare workers who earn less than that a week.
D. A conference on child care in the workplace which costs $200 may be too expensive to childcare workers who earn less than that on a weekly basis.

32. In accordance with estimates recently made, there are 40,000 to 50,000 nuclear weapons in our world today.   32.____
    A. Because of estimates recently, there are 40,000 to 50,000 nuclear weapons in the world today.
    B. In accordance with estimates made recently, there are 40,000 to 50,000 nuclear weapons in the world today.
    C. According to estimates made recently, there are 40,000 to 50,000 weapons in the world today.
    D. According to recent estimates, there are 40,000 to 50,000 nuclear weapons in the world today.

33. Motivation is important in problem solving, but they say   33.____
    that excessive motivation can inhibit the creative process.
    A. Motivation is important in problem solving, but, as they say, too much of it can inhibit the creative process.
    B. Motivation is important in problem solving and excessive motivation will inhibit the creative process.
    C. Motivation is important in problem solving, but excessive motivation can inhibit the creative process.
    D. Motivation is important in problem solving because excessive motivation can inhibit the creative process.

34. In selecting the best option calls for consulting with   34.____
    all the people that are involved in it.
    A. In selecting the best option consulting with all the people concerned with it.
    B. Calling for the best option, we consulted all the affected people.
    C. We called all the people involved to select the best option.
    D. To be sure of selecting the best option, one should consult all the people involved.

35. There are a number of problems with the following letter.   35.____
    From the options below, select the version that is MOST
    in accordance with standard business style, tone, and
    form.

Dear Sir:

We are so sorry that we have had to backorder your order for 15,000 widgets and 2,300 whatzits for such a long time. We have been having incredibly bad luck lately. When your order first came in no one could get to it because my secretary was out with the flu and her replacement didn't know what she was doing, then there was the dock strike in Cucamonga which held things up for awhile, and then it just somehow got lost. We think it may have fallen behind the radiator.

We are happy to say that all these problems have been taken care of, we are caught up on supplies, and we should have the stuff to you soon, in the near future -- about two weeks. You may not believe us after everything you've been through with us, but it's true.

We'll let you know as soon as we have a secure date for delivery. Thank you so much for continuing to do business with us after all the problems this probably has caused you.

Yours very sincerely,

Rob Barker

   A. Dear Sir:

      We are so sorry that we have had to backorder your order for 15,000 widgets and 2,300 whatzits. We have been having problems with staff lately and the dock strike hasn't helped anything.

      We are happy to say that all these problems have been taken care of. I've told my secretary to get right on it, and we should have the stuff to you soon. Thank you so much for continuing to do business with us after all the problems this must have caused you.

      We'll let you know as soon as we have a secure date for delivery.

      Sincerely,

      Rob Barker

   B. Dear Sir:

      We regret that we haven't been able to fill your order for 15,000 widgets and 2,300 whatzits in a timely fashion.

We'll let you know as soon as we have a secure date for delivery.

Sincerely,

Rob Barker

C. Dear Sir:

We are so very sorry that we haven't been able to fill your order for 15,000 widgets and 2,300 whatzits. We have been having incredibly bad luck lately, but things are much better now.

Thank you so much for bearing with us through all of this. We'll let you know as soon as we have a secure date for delivery.

Sincerely,

Rob Barker

D. Dear Sir:

We are very sorry that we haven't been able to fill your order for 15,000 widgets and 2,300 whatzits. Due to unforeseen difficulties, we have had to back-order your request. At this time, supplies have caught up to demand, and we foresee a delivery date within the next two weeks.

We'll let you know as soon as we have a secure date for delivery. Thank you for your patience.

Sincerely,

Rob Barker

KEY (CORRECT ANSWERS)

1. D	11. B	21. C	31. A
2. A	12. D	22. B	32. D
3. B	13. D	23. D	33. C
4. A	14. C	24. C	34. D
5. B	15. D	25. B	35. D
6. C	16. A	26. D	
7. B	17. A	27. A	
8. D	18. D	28. B	
9. A	19. D	29. C	
10. C	20. C	30. B	

ENGLISH GRAMMAR and USAGE
EXAMINATION SECTION

DIRECTIONS: In the passages that follow, certain words and phrases
are underlined and numbered. In each question, you
will find alternatives for each underlined part. You
are to choose the one that BEST expresses the idea,
makes the statement appropriate for standard written
English, or is worded MOST consistently with the style
and tone of the passage as a whole. Choose the alternative you consider BEST and write the letter in the space
at the right. If you think the original version is BEST,
choose NO CHANGE. Read each passage through once before
you begin to answer the questions that accompany it.
You cannot determine most answers without reading
several sentences beyond the phrase in question. Be sure
that you have read far enough ahead each time you choose
an alternative.

Questions 1-14.

DIRECTIONS: Questions 1 through 14 are based on the following passage.

Modern filmmaking had began in Paris in 1895 with the work of the
                   ‾‾‾‾‾‾‾‾‾
                       1
Lumière brothers.

Using their invention, the Cinématographe, the Lumières were able
          ‾‾‾‾‾‾‾‾‾‾‾‾‾‾‾‾‾‾‾‾‾‾‾‾‾‾‾‾
                         2
to photograph, print, and project moving pictures onto a screen. Their

films showed actual occurrences. A train approaching a station,
             ‾‾‾‾‾‾‾‾‾‾‾‾‾‾‾‾‾‾‾
                      3
people leaving a factory, workers demolishing a wall.

These early films had neither plot nor sound. But another French-

man, Georges Méliès, soon incorporated plot lines into his films. And
                                                    ‾‾‾‾
                                                     4
with his attempts to draw upon the potential of film to create fantasy

worlds. Méliès also was an early pioneer from special film effects.
‾‾‾‾‾‾   ‾‾‾‾‾‾‾‾‾‾‾‾‾‾‾‾‾‾‾‾‾‾‾‾‾‾
  5   6
Edwin S. Porter, an American filmmaker, took Méliès's emphasis on

narrative one step further. Believing that, continuity of shots was
                                       ‾‾‾‾‾‾‾‾‾‾‾‾‾‾‾‾‾‾‾‾‾‾‾
                                                  7
of primary importance in filmmaking, Porter connected images to
                                                        ‾‾‾‾‾‾‾‾‾
present, a sustained action. His GREAT TRAIN ROBBERY of 1903 opened
‾‾‾‾‾‾‾   8
a new era in film.

Because film was still considered as low entertainment in early
‾‾‾‾‾‾‾   ‾‾ ‾‾‾
  9   10
twentieth century America, it was on its way to becoming a respected

art form. Beginning in 1908, the American director D.W. Griffith discovered and explored techniques to make film a more expressive medium. With his technical contributions, <u>as well as</u> his attempts
<u> </u>
  11
to develop the intellectual and moral potential of film, Griffith helped build a solid foundation for the industry.

   <u>Thirty</u> years after the Lumière brothers' first show, sound
   12
<u>had yet been</u> added to the movies. Finally, in 1927, Hollywood pro-
   13
duced its first *talkie*, THE JAZZ SINGER. With sound, modern film <u>coming</u> of age.
   14

1. A. NO CHANGE   1.___
    B. begun
    C. began
    D. had some beginnings

2. A. NO CHANGE   2.___
    B. invention - the Cinématographe
    C. invention, the Cinématographe -
    D. invention, the Cinématographe

3. A. NO CHANGE   3.___
    B. actually occurrences, a
    C. actually occurrences - a
    D. actual occurrences: a

4. A. NO CHANGE   4.___
    B. about
    C. with
    D. to

5. A. NO CHANGE   5.___
    B. worlds,
    C. worlds; and
    D. worlds and

6. A. NO CHANGE   6.___
    B. pioneered
    C. pioneered the beginnings of
    D. pioneered the early beginnings of

7. A. NO CHANGE   7.___
    B. that continuity of shots
    C. that, continuity of shots,
    D. that continuity of shots

8. A. NO CHANGE
    B. images to present
    C. images and present
    D. images, and presenting

8.___

9. A. NO CHANGE
    B. (Begin new paragraph) In view of the fact that
    C. (Begin new paragraph) Although
    D. (Do NOT begin new paragraph) Since

9.___

10. A. NO CHANGE
    B. as if it were
    C. like it was
    D. OMIT the underlined portion

10.___

11. A. NO CHANGE
    B. similar to
    C. similar with
    D. like with

11.___

12. A. NO CHANGE
    B. (Begin new paragraph) Consequently, thirty
    C. (Do NOT begin new paragraph) Therefore, thirty
    D. (Do NOT begin new paragraph) As a consequence, thirty

12.___

13. A. NO CHANGE
    B. had yet to be
    C. has yet
    D. was yet being

13.___

14. A. NO CHANGE
    B. comes
    C. came
    D. had came

14.___

Questions 15-22.

DIRECTIONS: Questions 15 through 22 are based on the following passage.

One of the most awesome forces in nature is the tsunami, or tidal wave. A tsunami – the word is Japanese for harbor wave, can generate
                                                              15
the destructive power of many atomic bombs.

Tsunamis usually appear in a series of four or five waves about
          16
fifteen minutes apart. They begin deep in the ocean, gather remarkable speed as they travel, and cover great distances. The wave triggered by the explosion of Krakatoa in 1883 circled the world in three days.

Tsunamis being known to sink large ships at sea, they are most
        17
dangerous when they reach land. Close to shore, an oncoming tsunami

is forced upward and skyward, perhaps as high as 100 feet. This
                18
combination of height and speed accounts for the tsunami's great power.

    That *tsunami* is a Japanese word is no accident, due to the fact th
                                                      19
no nation frequently has been so visited by giant waves as Japan.
          20
Tsunamis reach that country regularly, and with devastating consequence
    21
One Japanese tsunami flattened several towns in 1896, also killed 27,00
                                                     22
people.

15. A. NO CHANGE   15.___
     B. tsunami, the word is Japanese for harbor wave -
     C. tsunami - the word is Japanese for harbor wave -
     D. tsunami - the word being Japanese for harbor wave,

16. A. NO CHANGE   16.___
     B. (Begin new paragraph) Consequently, tsunamis
     C. (Do NOT begin new paragraph) Tsunamis consequently
     D. (Do NOT begin new paragraph) Yet, tsunamis

17. A. NO CHANGE   17.___
     B. Because tsunamis have been
     C. Although tsunamis have been
     D. Tsunamis have been

18. A. NO CHANGE   18.___
     B. upward to the sky,
     C. upward in the sky,
     D. upward,

19. A. NO CHANGE   19.___
     B. when one takes into consideration the fact that
     C. seeing as how
     D. for

20. A. NO CHANGE   20.___
     B. (Place after *has*)
     C. (Place after *so*)
     D. (Place after *visited*)

21. A. NO CHANGE   21.___
     B. Moreover, tsunamis
     C. However, tsunamis
     D. Because tsunamis

22. A. NO CHANGE
     B. 1896 and killed 27,000 people.
     C. 1896 and killing 27,000 people.
     D. 1896, and 27,000 people as well.

22.____

Questions 23-33.

DIRECTIONS: Questions 23 through 33 are based on the following passage.

I was married one August on a farm in Maine. The ceremony, itself,
         _____   _____
            23   24
taking place in an arbor of pine boughs we had built and constructed in
_____   _____
                                                    25
the yard next to the house. On the morning of the wedding day, we

parked the tractors behind the shed, have tied the dogs to an oak tree
                                     _____
                                        26
to keep them from chasing the guests, and put the cows out to pasture.

We had thought of everything, it seemed. Thus we had forgotten how
                                           ____
                                            27
interested a cow can be in what is going on around them. During the
                                            _____
                                               28
ceremony, my sister (who has taken several years of lessons) was to
                    _____
                                     29
play a flute solo. We were all listening intently when she had began
                                                              _____
                                                                 30
to play. As the first notes reached us, we were surprised to hear a

bass line under the flute's treble melody. Looking around, the source
                                                             _____
                                                                 31
was quickly discovered. There was Star, my pet Guernsey, her head
_____
hanging over the pasture fence, mooing along with the delicate strains

of Bach.

Star took our laughter as being like a compliment, and we took
                       _____
                            32
her contribution that way, too. It was a sign of approval - the kind
                                 _____
                                   33
you would find only at a farm wedding.

23. A. NO CHANGE
     B. married, one
     C. married on an
     D. married, in an

23.____

24. A. NO CHANGE
     B. ceremony itself taking
     C. ceremony itself took
     D. ceremony, itself took

24.____

25.   A. NO CHANGE
      B. which had been built and constructed
      C. we had built and constructed it
      D. we had built
                                      25.___

26.   A. NO CHANGE
      B. tie
      C. tied
      D. tying
                                      26.___

27.   A. NO CHANGE
      B. (Do NOT begin new paragraph) And
      C. (Begin new paragraph) But
      D. (Begin new paragraph) Moreover,
                                      27.___

28.   A. NO CHANGE
      B. around her.
      C. in her own vicinity.
      D. in their immediate area.
                                      28.___

29.   A. NO CHANGE
      B. (whom has taken many years of lessons)
      C. (who has been trained in music)
      D. OMIT the underlined portion
                                      29.___

30.   A. NO CHANGE
      B. begun
      C. began
      D. would begin
                                      30.___

31.   A. NO CHANGE
      B. the discovery of the source was quick.
      C. the discovery of the source was quickly made.
      D. we quickly discovered the source.
                                      31.___

32.   A. NO CHANGE
      B. as
      C. just as
      D. as if
                                      32.___

33.   A. NO CHANGE
      B. Yet it was
      C. But it was
      D. Being
                                      33.___

Questions 34-42.

DIRECTIONS: Questions 34 through 42 are based on the following passage.

Riding a bicycle in Great Britain is not the same as riding a bicycle in the United States. Americans bicycling in Britain will find some <u>basic fundamental</u> differences in the rules of the road and in the
34
attitudes of motorists.

<u>Probably</u> most difficult for the American cyclist is adjusting <u>with</u>
35   36
British traffic patterns. <u>Knowing that traffic</u> in Britain moves on
37
the left-hand side of the road, bicycling <u>once</u> there is the mirror
38
image of what it is in the United States.

The problem of adjusting to traffic patterns is somewhat lessened,
<u>however,</u> by the respect with which British motorists treat bicyclists.
39
A cyclist in a traffic circle, for example, is given the same right-of-
way <u>with</u> the driver of any other vehicle. However, the cyclist is
40
expected to obey the rules of the road. This <u>difference in the American</u>
41
<u>and British attitudes toward bicyclists</u> may stem from differing
41
attitudes toward the bicycle itself. Whereas Americans frequently
view bicycles as <u>toys, but</u> the British treat them primarily as vehicles.
42

34. A. NO CHANGE   34.___
     B. basic and fundamental
     C. basically fundamental
     D. basic

35. A. NO CHANGE   35.___
     B. Even so, probably
     C. Therefore, probably
     D. As a result, probably

36. A. NO CHANGE   36.___
     B. upon
     C. on
     D. to

37. A. NO CHANGE   37.___
     B. Seeing that traffic
     C. Because traffic
     D. Traffic

38. A. NO CHANGE
     B. once you are
     C. once one is
     D. OMIT the underlined portion

38.___

39. A. NO CHANGE
     B. also,
     C. moreover,
     D. therefore,

39.___

40. A. NO CHANGE
     B. as
     C. as if
     D. as with

40.___

41. A. NO CHANGE
     B. difference in the American and British attitudes
        toward bicyclists
     C. difference, in the American and British attitudes
        toward bicyclists
     D. difference in the American, and British, attitudes
        toward bicyclists

41.___

42. A. NO CHANGE
     B. toys;
     C. toys,
     D. toys; but

42.___

Questions 43-51.

DIRECTIONS: Questions 43 through 51 are based on the following passage

People have always believed that supernatural powers tend toward
                                                              43
some influence on lives for good or for ill. Superstition originated
with the idea that individuals could in turn, exert influence at
                                     44   45
spirits. Certain superstitions are so deeply embedded in our culture
                                      46
that intelligent people sometimes act in accordance with them.

One common superstitious act is knocking on wood after boasting
of good fortune. People once believed that gods inhabited trees and,
therefore, were present in the wood used to build houses. Fearing
that speaking of good luck within the gods' hearing might anger
them, people knocked on wood to deafen the gods and avoid their dis-
    47
pleasure.

Another superstitious <u>custom and practice</u> is throwing salt over
the left shoulder. <u>Considering</u> salt was once considered sacred,
people thought that spilling it brought bad luck. Since right and
left represented good and evil, the believers used their right hands,
which symbolized good, to throw a pinch of salt over their left
shoulders into the eyes of the evil gods. <u>Because of this,</u> people
attempted to avert misfortune.

Without realizing the origin of superstitions, many people
exhibit superstitious behavior. <u>Others avoid</u> walking under ladders
and stepping on cracks in sidewalks, without having any idea why
they are doing so.

43. A. NO CHANGE   43.____
    B. can influence
    C. tend to influence on
    D. are having some influence on

44. A. NO CHANGE   44.____
    B. could, turning,
    C. could, in turn,
    D. could, in turn

45. A. NO CHANGE   45.____
    B. of
    C. toward
    D. on

46. A. NO CHANGE   46.____
    B. so deep embedded
    C. deepest embedded
    D. embedded deepest

47. A. NO CHANGE   47.____
    B. them; people
    C. them: some people
    D. them, they

48. A. NO CHANGE   48.____
    B. custom
    C. traditional custom
    D. customary habit

49. A. NO CHANGE
    B. Although
    C. Because
    D. Keeping in mind that

49. ___

50. A. NO CHANGE
    B. As a result of this,
    C. Consequently,
    D. In this way,

50. ___

51. A. NO CHANGE
    B. Often avoiding
    C. Avoiding
    D. They avoid

51. ___

Questions 52-66.

DIRECTIONS: Questions 52 through 66 are based on the following passage

In the 1920s, the Y.M.C.A. sponsored one of the first programs

in order to promote more enlightened public opinion on racial matters;
         52

the organization started special university classes in which young
                                                     53

people could study race relations. Among the guest speakers invited

to conduct the sessions, one of the most popular was George Washington

Carver, the scientist from Tuskegee Institute.

As a student, Carver himself had been active in the Y.M.C.A.

He shared its evangelical and educational philosophy. However, in
   54

1923, the Y.M.C.A. arranged Carver's first initial speaking tour, the
 55   56

scientist accepted with apprehension. He was to speak at several

white colleges, most of whose students had never seen, let alone heard,

an educated black man.

Although Carver's appearances did sometimes cause occasional
                               57

controversy, but his quiet dedication prevailed, and his humor quickly
          58

won over his audiences. Nevertheless, for the next decade, Carver
                         59

toured the Northeast, Midwest, and South under Y.M.C.A. sponsorship.
                                                            60

Speaking at places never before open to blacks. On these tours

Carver befriended thousands of students, many of whom subsequently
                                                   61

corresponded with his <u>afterwards.</u>
           62

    The <u>tours, unfortunately were</u> not without discomfort for Carver.
             63

There were the indignities of *Jim Crow* accommodations and racial

insults from strangers. <u>As a result,</u> the scientist's enthusiasm never
                 64

faltered. <u>Avoiding any discussion of</u> the political and social aspects
             65

of racial injustice; instead, Carver conducted his whole life as an

indirect attack <u>to</u> prejudice. This, as much as his science, is his
           66

legacy to humankind.

52. A. NO CHANGE   52.___
      B. to promote
      C. for the promoting of what is
      D. for the promotion of what are

53. A. NO CHANGE   53.___
      B. from which
      C. that
      D. by which

54. A. NO CHANGE   54.___
      B. Sharing
      C. Having shared
      D. Because he shared

55. A. NO CHANGE   55.___
      B. 1923
      C. 1923, and
      D. 1923, when

56. A. NO CHANGE   56.___
      B. Carvers' first, initial
      C. Carvers first initial
      D. Carver's first

57. A. NO CHANGE   57.___
      B. sometimes did
      C. did
      D. OMIT the underlined portion

58. A. NO CHANGE   58.___
      B. controversy and
      C. controversy,
      D. controversy, however

59. A. NO CHANGE   59.___
      B. However, for
      C. However, from
      D. For

60. A. NO CHANGE   60.___
     B. sponsorship and spoke
     C. sponsorship; and spoke
     D. sponsorship, and speaking

61. A. NO CHANGE   61.___
     B. who
     C. them
     D. those

62. A. NO CHANGE   62.___
     B. later.
     C. sometime later.
     D. OMIT the underlined portion and end the sentence with
         a period

63. A. NO CHANGE   63.___
     B. tours, unfortunately, were
     C. tours unfortunately, were
     D. tours, unfortunately, are

64. A. NO CHANGE   64.___
     B. So
     C. But
     D. Therefore,

65. A. NO CHANGE   65.___
     B. He avoided discussing
     C. Having avoided discussing
     D. Upon avoiding the discussion of

66. A. NO CHANGE   66.___
     B. over
     C. on
     D. of

Questions 67-75.

DIRECTIONS: Questions 67 through 75 are based on the following passage

Shooting rapids is not the only way to experience the thrill of
canoeing. An ordinary-looking stream, innocent of rocks and white
         ‾‾
         67
water, can provide adventure, as long as it has three essential

features; a swift current, close banks, and has plenty of twists and
‾‾‾‾‾‾‾‾   ‾‾‾
   68   69
turns.

A powerful current causes tension, for canoeists know they will
‾
70
have only seconds for executing the maneuvers necessary to prevent

crashing into the trees lining the narrow <u>streams banks.</u> Of course,
71

the <u>narrowness, itself, being</u> crucial in creating the tension. On a
72

broad stream, canoeists can pause frequently, catch their breath,

and get their bearings. However, <u>to</u> a narrow stream, where every
73

minute <u>you run</u> the risk of being knocked down by a low-hanging tree
74

limb, they must be constantly alert. Yet even the fast current and

close banks would be manageable if the stream were fairly straight.

The expenditure of energy required to paddle furiously, first on one

side of the canoe and then on the other, wearies <u>both the nerves as</u>
75

<u>well as the body.</u>

67. A. NO CHANGE   67.____
     B. They say that for adventure an
     C. Many finding that an
     D. The old saying that an

68. A. NO CHANGE   68.____
     B. features:
     C. features,
     D. features; these being

69. A. NO CHANGE   69.____
     B. there must be
     C. with
     D. OMIT the underlined portion

70. A. NO CHANGE   70.____
     B. Thus, a
     C. Therefore, a
     D. Furthermore, a

71. A. NO CHANGE   71.____
     B. stream's banks.
     C. streams bank's.
     D. banks of the streams.

72. A. NO CHANGE   72.____
     B. narrowness, itself is
     C. narrowness itself is
     D. narrowness in itself being

73. A. NO CHANGE   73.____
     B. near
     C. on
     D. with

74. A. NO CHANGE
    B. the canoer runs
    C. one runs
    D. they run
                                              74.___

75. A. NO CHANGE
    B. the nerves as well as the body
    C. the nerves, also, as well as the body
    D. not only the body but also the nerves as well
                                              75.___

KEY (CORRECT ANSWERS)

1. C	26. C	51. D
2. A	27. C	52. B
3. D	28. B	53. A
4. A	29. D	54. A
5. B	30. C	55. D
6. B	31. D	56. D
7. D	32. B	57. C
8. B	33. A	58. C
9. C	34. D	59. D
10. D	35. A	60. B
11. A	36. D	61. A
12. A	37. C	62. D
13. B	38. D	63. B
14. C	39. A	64. C
15. C	40. B	65. B
16. A	41. A	66. C
17. C	42. C	67. A
18. D	43. B	68. B
19. D	44. C	69. D
20. C	45. D	70. A
21. A	46. A	71. B
22. B	47. A	72. C
23. A	48. B	73. C
24. C	49. C	74. D
25. D	50. D	75. B

EXAMINATION SECTION
TEST 1

DIRECTIONS: Each of the following sentences, as written, is grammatically incorrect for one or more reasons. Rewrite the sentences in CORRECT grammatical form, making as few changes as possible from the original text.

1. I did not know how to reply when he wanted to know was I going to assist him in the undertaking.

2. You will observe not only the rules in the book, but you will use your common sense as well.

3. The change in his condition is distinctly for the better due to the hard work of the doctor and the nurse.

4. If he will come before I leave, I will give him your message.

5. Hitch your wagon to a star and ride, ride till the sun.

6. The judge declared that neither the policeman nor the man whom he had arrested were telling the whole truth.

7. The reason why the sunspots cause changes in the weather is because they are electric disturbances.

8. Bring this book to the library in order that you will not have to pay an accumulated fine.

9. He had laid so long in bed that he found it difficult to move about normally.

10. He wanted us to slowly and carefully pour the oil into the smaller bottles.

———

KEY (CORRECT ANSWERS)

1. I did not know how to reply when he wanted to know whether I was going to assist him in the undertaking.

2. Not only will you observe the rules in the book, but you will use your common sense as well.

3. The change in his condition is distinctly for the better because of the hard work of the doctor and the nurse.

4. If he comes before I leave, I will give him your message.

5. Hitch your wagon to a star and ride, ride to the sun.

6. The judge declared that neither the policeman nor the man whom he had arrested was telling the whole truth.

7. The reason why the sunspots cause changes in the weather is that they are electric disturbances.

8. Take this book to the library in order that you will not have to pay an accumulated fine.

9. He had lain so long in bed that he found it difficult to move about normally.

10. He wanted us to pour the oil slowly and carefully into the smaller bottles.

TEST 2

DIRECTIONS: Each of the following sentences, as written, is grammatically incorrect for one or more reasons. Rewrite the sentences in CORRECT grammatical form, making as few changes as possible from the original text.

1. We could not be sure if he meant to be present or was just politely suggesting that he might come.

2. They tell me that the coaches invite only such members of the freshman class who are apt to prove good material in their upper years.

3. We found less persons on the beach after the storm than at any other time.

4. We asked permission to partake in the activities, but we were refused.

5. Appreciating our good luck, the play for which we had received free tickets, seemed doubly interesting.

6. The book he recommended was different than the one you bought for me.

7. Thousands and thousands of young men and women graduate our colleges annually.

8. One can never say that the person whom you know is a friend of yours one day, will be your friend the next.

9. Their's not to reason why is a famous quote from a poem by Tennyson.

10. If not for his father's timely advice, he would have left school.

———

KEY (CORRECT ANSWERS)

1. We could not be sure whether he meant to be present or was just politely suggesting that he might come.

2. They tell me that the coaches invite only such members of the freshman class as are apt to prove good material in their upper years.

3. We found fewer persons on the beach after the storm than at any other time.

4. We asked permission to take part in the activities, but we were refused.

5. Since we appreciated our good luck, the play for which we had received free tickets seemed doubly interesting.

6. The book he recommended was different from the one you bought for me.

7. Thousands and thousands of young men and women are graduated from our colleges annually.

8. One can never say that the person who you know is your friend today, will be your friend tomorrow.

9. Theirs not to reason why is a famous quotation from a poem by Tennyson.

10. Had it not been for his father's timely advice, he would have left school.

TEST 3

DIRECTIONS: Each of the following sentences, as written, is grammatically incorrect for one or more reasons. Rewrite the sentences in CORRECT grammatical form, making as few changes as possible from the original text.

1. He went to the concert so often before, that he did not care to go that night.

2. Although he claimed that all his jewels and cash had been robbed, he did not seem to be the least bit worried.

3. Well what are you going to do now without your equipment and gear.

4. Let us all get the true facts first; then we can reach a decision.

5. We bought a book suitable for you, but which I would not think of reading.

6. While waiting for my friend to appear, a telephone message from him arrived.

7. He certainly deserves to be punished: still and all I feel sorry for him.

8. Cheating on an examination is as foolish as to conceal your symptoms from the doctor.

9. I consider aviation a very hazardous occupation, but being that you have set your heart on learning how to fly, I shall say no more in regard(s) to your decision.

10. Her appearance was not only striking, but she had an interesting personality as well.

———

KEY (CORRECT ANSWERS)

1. He had gone to the concert so often before that he did not care to go that night.

2. Although he claimed that all his jewels and cash had been stolen, he did not seem to be the least bit worried.

3. Well, what are you going to do now without your equipment and gear?

4. Let us all get the facts first; then we can reach a decision.

5. We bought a book suitable for you but one which I would not think of reading.

6. While I was waiting for my friend to appear, a telephone message from him arrived.

7. He certainly deserves to be punished; nevertheless, I feel sorry for him.

8. Cheating on an examination is as foolish as concealing your symptoms from the doctor.

9. I consider aviation a very hazardous occupation, but since you have set your heart on learning how to fly, I shall say no more in regard to your decision.

10. Not only was her appearance striking, but she had an interesting personality as well.

TEST 4

DIRECTIONS: Each of the following sentences, as written, is grammatically incorrect for one or more reasons. Rewrite the sentences in CORRECT grammatical form, making as few changes as possible from the original text.

1. Walking up Broadway from Fulton Street, the Woolworth Building strikes the observer.

2. Imagine a person risking his life to so dramatically save the day.

3. We expect to go irregardless of the weather clearing up.

4. The jar was so full that he had to spill some of the water in the sink.

5. George Washington the man who everyone admires was keenly alive to every opportunity.

6. Queen Elizabeth as the story goes was once very much in love with Essex.

7. The Nebular Hypothesis LaPlace's famous theory is not universally accepted.

8. The crew had no sooner removed the last passenger when the ship sunk.

9. Whom do you expect him to be was the question put to the defendant.

10. You said you should probably go by train.

———

KEY (CORRECT ANSWERS)

1. As he walks up Broadway from Fulton Street, the Woolworth Building strikes the observer.

2. Imagine a person's risking his life to save the day so dramatically.

3. We expect to go regardless of the weather clearing up.

4. The jar was so full that we had to pour some of the water into the sink.

5. George Washington, the man whom everyone admires, was keenly alive to every opportunity.

6. Queen Elizabeth, as the story goes, was once very much in love with Essex.

7. The Nebular Hypothesis, La Place's famous theory, is not universally accepted.

8. The crew had no sooner removed the last passenger than the ship sank.

9. "Whom do you expect him to be?" was the question put to the defendant.

10. You said you would probably go by train.

———

TEST 5

DIRECTIONS: Each of the following sentences, as written, is grammatically incorrect for one or more reasons. Rewrite the sentence in CORRECT grammatical form, making as few changes as possible from the original text.

1. The rotation plan is used in office practice classes, largely due to the fact that there is insufficient equipment.

2. This calls for the purchase of a large number of machines which is practically impossible from an economy standpoint.

3. The advantages of such an arrangement enables the teacher to plan her work more efficiently.

4. There is a stigma attached to being in a slow group and danger of pupils in a bright group from becoming conceited.

5. There are administrative details that can only be worked out with the sympathetic cooperation of the principal.

6. For instance if there were only an average and a bright class, the slow pupils would be put into the average.

7. Pupils and parents would object to a child being classified "slow". This has not been difficult to overcome where the plan has been tried.

8. The second and third Epistle of John contain each a single chapter.

9. It boils down to this: either you or I are right.

10. No time, no money, no labor was spared to make the fair an artistic success.

———

KEY (CORRECT ANSWERS)

1. The rotation plan is used in office practice classes largely because of the fact that there is insufficient equipment.

2. This calls for the purchase of a large number of machines. Such a purchase is practically impossible from an economy standpoint.

3. The advantages of such an arrangement is that it enables the teacher to plan her work more efficiently.

4. There is a stigma attached to being in a slow group and a danger that the pupils in a bright group might become conceited.

5. There are administrative details that can be worked out only with the sympathetic cooperation of the principal.

6. For instance, if there were only an average and a bright class, the slow pupils would be put into the average class.

7. Pupils and parents would object to a child's being classified "slow." This has not been difficult to overcome when the plan has been tried.

8. Each of the second and third Epistles of John consists of a single chapter.

9. It boils down to this: either you or I am right.

10. No time, no money, no labor were spared to make the fair an artistic one.

———

TEST 6

DIRECTIONS: Each of the following sentences, as written, is grammatically incorrect for one or more reasons. Rewrite the sentence in CORRECT grammatical form, making as few changes as possible from the original text.

1. Bread is more nutritious, but not so cheap, as potatoes.

2. This dedication may serve for almost any book that has, is, or may be published.

3. Mr. Asquith concluded on a note of high appeal for the substitution of the Supreme Council by the League of Nations.

4. The municipality purchased these articles in wholesale quantities and it was to the Town Hall that people applied for them and were served by municipal employees.

5. There is a distinction between the man who gives with conviction and he who is simply buying a title.

6. Because his manners were exceptionable he was invited most every where by the elite of the town.

7. If I'd have gone about collecting this data as quick as you desired, the job would now be finished.

8. Inside of a week the thieves broke in his house twice.

9. Don't be angry at me for losing your book; this one is as new or newer than yours.

10. It was none other but Morgan; the reason he left so suddenly was because he feared the discovery of the plot.

―――

KEY (CORRECT ANSWERS)

1. Bread is more nutritious than potatoes but not so cheap.

2. This dedication may serve for almost any book that has been or may be published.

3. Mr. Asquith concluded on a high note of appeal for the substitution of the Supreme Council by the League of Nations.

4. The municipality purchased these articles in wholesale quantities, and it was at the Town Hall that people applied for them and were served by municipal employees.

5. There is a distinction between the man who gives with conviction and him who is simply buying a title.

6. Because his manners were unexceptionable he was invited almost everywhere by the elite of the town.

7. If I had gone about collecting these data as quickly as you desired, the job would now be finished.

8. Within a week the thieves broke into his house twice.

9. Don't be angry at me for losing your book; this one is as new as or newer than yours.

10. It was none other than Morgan; the reason he left so suddenly was that he feared the discovery of the plot.

———

TEST 7

DIRECTIONS: Each of the following sentences, as written, is grammatically incorrect for one or more reasons. Rewrite the sentence in CORRECT grammatical form, making as few changes as possible from the original text.

1. Due to his poor management, I found conditions different to what I expected, even though he was enamored by his work.

2. One need not take examinations preliminary for college entrance, providing your scholastic record is high enough to exempt you from them.

3. I do not like this passage, but leave it stay in the examination.

4. A duel is when two persons fight to settle a quarrel that has risen according to certain rules.

5. "Will you be glad to see us?" He had ought to know what my answer would be.

6. A big gray cat dashed across the road.

7. We saw many wonderful things for example, a carved sun dial.

8. By August he shall be living in New York for ten years.

9. Madame Curie was the cleverest of most women of her time.

10. If the book is laying on my desk, will you send it to the library for me, please?

———

KEY (CORRECT ANSWERS)

1. Because of his poor management, I found conditions different from what I had expected, even though he was enamored of his work.

2. One need not take preliminary examinations for college entrance, provided that your scholastic record is high enough to exempt you from them.

3. I do not like this passage, but let it stay in the examination.

4. A duel occurs when two persons fight according to certain rules to settle a quarrel that has arisen.

5. "Shall you be glad to see us?" He ought to have known what my answer would be.

6. A big, gray cat dashed across the road.

7. We saw many wonderful things; for example, a carved sun dial.

8. By August he will have lived in New York ten years.

9. Madame Curie was cleverer than most women of her time.

10. If the book is lying on my desk, will you send it to the library for me, please?

———

TEST 8

DIRECTIONS: Each of the following sentences, as written, is grammatically incorrect for one or more reasons. Rewrite the sentences in CORRECT grammatical form, making as few changes as possible from the original text.

1. It is an insult to I who am your friend.

2. Every one of the spectators were ready to declare they thought it cruel.

3. We passed over the road quickly and soon the camp was reached.

4. He is almost the handsomest man I ever saw.

5. The person who steals in nine cases out of ten is driven by hunger.

6. He is one of the greatest, if not the greatest lawyers of America.

7. John as well as his brother is going to the party.

8. The storm was already at hand, I had no time to eat.

9. Dr. Brown, who was to be here yesterday, left a prescription for me.

10. He bought nails, bolts, locks, and etc.

KEY (CORRECT ANSWERS)

1. It is an insult to me who am your friend.

2. Every one of the spectators was ready to declare he thought it cruel.

3. We passed over the road quickly and soon reached the camp.

4. He is perhaps the handsomest man I have ever seen.

5. The person who steals is, in nine cases out of ten, driven by hunger.

6. He is one of the greatest lawyers of America, if not the greatest.

7. John, as well as his brother, is going to the party.

8. The storm was already at hand: I had no time to eat.

9. Dr. Brown, who was here yesterday, left a prescription for me.

10. He bought nails, bolts, locks, etc.

TEST 9

DIRECTIONS: Each of the following sentences, as written, is grammatically incorrect for one or more reasons. Rewrite the sentences in CORRECT grammatical form, making as few changes as possible from the original text.

1. I like books on the whole, but these kind of books always bores me.

2. Is there any chance of you leaving the city this summer?

3. Many important events had happened since I wrote that news article.

4. I lie awake all night thinking of the future.

5. He admitted those only with tickets.

6. Favored by a warm winter climate, I regard Florida as a popular resort.

7. After hearing modern jazz, all other music sounds dull.

8. He has two friends to help him now, John and she.

9. This pen may be carried by anyone, everywhere, without danger of it leaking.

10. It was easiest to purchase gifts for her than me.

KEY (CORRECT ANSWERS)

1. I like books on the whole, but this kind of book always bores me.

2. Is there any chance of your leaving the city this summer?

3. Many important events have happened since I wrote that news article.

4. I lay awake all night thinking of the future.

5. He admitted only those with tickets.

6. Favored by a warm winter climate, Florida is a popular resort.

7. After hearing modern jazz, I feel that all other music sounds dull.

8. He has two friends to help him now, John and her.

9. This pen may be carried by anyone, everywhere, without danger of its leaking.

10. It was easier to purchase gifts for her than me.

———

TEST 10

DIRECTIONS: Each of the following sentences, as written, is grammatically incorrect for one or more reasons. Rewrite the sentences in CORRECT grammatical form, making as few changes as possible from the original text.

1. The book is about a peddler whom all the Americans thought was an English spy.

2. Bad news travel fast.

3. We must strive to attain academic freedom irregardless of personal consequences.

4. He promised that he might deliver the car on September first, but he did not say which year.

5. You must proceed slow with difficult experiments.

6. They advise others to take the same course that they have.

7. Without noticing, they ride past their station.

8. If I was you, I should wait for them.

9. That he is wrong, he already knows.

10. The richness of his apparel and arms were conspicuous.

———

KEY (CORRECT ANSWERS)

1. The book is about a peddler who all the Americans thought was an English spy.

2. Bad news travels fast.

3. We must strive to attain academic freedom regardless of personal consequences.

4. He promised that he would deliver the car on September first, but he did not say which year.

5. You must proceed slowly with difficult experiments.

6. They advised others to take the same course that they had taken.

7. Without noticing, they rode past their station.

8. If I were you, I should wait for them.

9. That he was wrong, he already knows.

10. The richness of his apparel and arms was conspicuous.

———

English Expression

DIRECTIONS FOR THIS SECTION:
   Each question or incomplete statement is followed by several suggested answers or completions. Select the one that *BEST* answers the question or completes the statement. *PRINT THE LETTER OF THE CORRECT ANSWER IN THE SPACE AT THE RIGHT.*

TEST

Questions 1-9.
DIRECTIONS: The following sentences contain problems in grammar, usage diction (choice of words), and idiom.
      Some sentences are correct.
      No sentence contains more than one error.
You will find that the error, if there is one, is underlined and lettered. Assume that all other elements of the sentence are correct and cannot be changed. In choosing answers, follow the requirements of standard written English. If there is an error, select the *one underlined part* that must be changed in order to make the sentence correct.
If there is no error, mark answer space E.

1. In planning your future, one must be as honest with your-
        A   B
   self as possible, make careful decisions about the best
   course to follow to achieve a particular purpose, and,
                  C
   above all, have the courage to stand by those decisions.
                                   D
   No error.
   E
                                                              1. ...

2. Even though history does not actually repeat itself,
   A
   knowledge of history can give current problems a familiar,
            B   C
   less formidable look. No error.
   D   E
                                                              2. ...

3. The Curies had almost exhausted their resources, and
                 A
   for a time it seemed unlikely that they ever would find
            B   C
   the solvent to their financial problems. No error.
      D   E
                                                              3. ...

4. If the rumors are correct, Deane will not be convicted,
      A   B
   for each of the officers on the court realizes that
   Colson and Holdman may be the real culprit and that their
                             C   D
   testimony is not completely trustworthy. No error.
                                             E
                                                              4. ...

5. The citizens of Washington, like Los Angeles, prefer to
                                A
   commute by automobile, even though motor vehicles contribute nearly as many contaminants to the air as do all other
       B   C
   sources combined. No error.
           D   E
                                                              5. ...

1

6. By the time Robert Vasco completes his testimony, every   6. ...
                   A

   major executive of our company but Ray Ashurst and I
                                             B

   will have been accused of complicity in the stock swindle.
         C   D
   No error.
       E

7. Within six months the store was operating   7. ...
       A

   profitably and efficient; shelves were well stocked,
           B   C

   goods were selling rapidly, and the cash register
   was ringing constantly. No error.
         D   E

8. Shakespeare's comedies have an advantage over Shaw   8. ...
                                       A

   in that Shakespeare's were written primarily to entertain
           B   C

   and not to argue for a cause. No error.
       D   E

9. Any true insomniac is well aware of the futility of   9. ...
                     A

   such measures as drinking hot milk,
           B

   regular hours, deep breathing, counting sheep, and
                C

   concentrating on black velvet. No error.
         D   E

Questions 10-15.

DIRECTIONS: In each of the following sentences, some part of the sentence or the entire sentence is underlined. Beneath each sentence you will find five ways of phrasing the underlined part. The first of these repeats the original; the other four are different. If you think the original is better than any of the alternatives, choose answer A; otherwise choose one of the others. Select the best version and print the letter of the correct answer in the space at the right. This is a test of correctness and effectiveness of expression. In choosing answers, follow the requirements of standard written English; that is, pay attention to grammar, choice of words, sentence construction, and punctuation. Choose the answer that produces the most effective sentence - clear and exact, without awkwardness or ambiguity. Do not make a choice that changes the meaning of the original sentence.

10. The tribe of warriors believed that boys and girls should   10. ...
    be reared separate, and, as soon as he was weaned, the boys
    were taken from their mothers.

    A. reared separate, and, as soon as he was weaned, the
       boys were taken from their mothers
    B. reared separate, and, as soon as he was weaned, a boy
       was taken from his mother
    C. reared separately, and, as soon as he was weaned, the
       boys were taken from their mothers
    D. reared separately, and, as soon as a boy was weaned,
       they were taken from their mothers
    E. reared separately, and, as soon as a boy was weaned,
       he was taken from his mother

2

11. <u>Despite Vesta being only the third largest, it is by</u>   11. ...
<u>far the brightest of the known asteroids</u>.
    A. Despite Vesta being only the third largest, it is
       by far the brightest of the known asteroids.
    B. Vesta, though only the third largest asteroid, is
       by far the brightest of the known ones.
    C. Being only the third largest, yet Vesta is by far
       the brightest of the known asteroids.
    D. Vesta, though only the third largest of the known
       asteroids, is by far the brightest.
    E. Vesta is only the third largest of the asteroids,
       it being, however, the brightest one.

12. As a result of the discovery of the Dead Sea Scrolls, our   12. ...
understanding of the roots of Christianity <u>has had to be</u>
<u>revised considerably</u>.
    A. has had to be revised considerably
    B. have had to be revised considerably
    C. has had to undergo revision to a considerable degree
    D. have had to be subjected to considerable revision
    E. has had to be revised in a considerable way

13. Because <u>it is imminently suitable to</u> dry climates, adobe   13. ...
has been a traditional building material throughout the
southwestern states.
    A. it is imminently suitable to
    B. it is eminently suitable for
    C. it is eminently suitable when in
    D. of its eminent suitability with
    E. of being imminently suitable in

14. <u>Martell is more concerned with demonstrating that racial</u>   14. ...
<u>prejudice exists than preventing it from doing harm, which</u>
<u>explains</u> why his work is not always highly regarded.
    A. Martell is more concerned with demonstrating that
       racial prejudice exists than preventing it from doing
       harm, which explains
    B. Martell is more concerned with demonstrating that
       racial prejudice exists than with preventing it from
       doing harm, and this explains
    C. Martell is more concerned with demonstrating that
       racial prejudice exists than with preventing it from
       doing harm, an explanation of
    D. Martell's greater concern for demonstrating that racial
       prejudice exists than preventing it from doing harm -
       this explains
    E. Martell's greater concern for demonstrating that racial
       prejudice exists than for preventing it from doing harm
       explains

15. <u>Throughout this history of the American West there runs a</u>   15. ...
<u>steady commentary on the deception and mistreatment of the</u>
<u>Indians</u>.
    A. Throughout this history of the American West there runs
       a steady commentary on the deception and mistreatment of
       the Indians.
    B. There is a steady commentary provided on the deception
       and mistreatment of the Indians and it runs throughout
       this history of the American West.

3

C. The deception and mistreatment of the Indians provide a steady comment that runs throughout this history of the American West.

D. Comment on the deception and mistreatment of the Indians is steadily provided and runs throughout this history of the American West.

E. Running throughout this history of the American West is a steady commentary that is provided on the deception and mistreatment of the Indians.

Questions 16-20.

DIRECTIONS: In each of the following questions you are given a complete sentence to be rephrased according to the directions which follow it. You should rephrase the sentence mentally to save time, although you may make notes in your test book if you wish.

Below each sentence and its directions are listed words or phrases that may occur in your revised sentence. When you have thought out a good sentence, look in the choices A through E for the word or entire phrase that is included in your revised sentence, and print the letter of the correct answer in the space at the right. The word or phrase you choose should be the most accurate and most nearly complete of all the choices given, and should be part of a sentence that meets the requirements of standard written English.

Of course, a number of different sentences can be obtained if the sentence is revised according to directions, and not all of these possibilities can be included in only five choices. If you should find that you have thought of a sentence that contains none of the words or phrases listed in the choices, you should attempt to rephrase the sentence again so that it includes a word or phrase that is listed. Although the directions may at times require you to change the relationship between parts of the sentence or to make slight changes in meaning in other ways, make only those changes that the directions require; that is, keep the meaning the same, or as nearly the same as the directions permit. If you think that more than one good sentence can be made according to the directions, select the sentence that is most exact, effective, and natural in phrasing and construction.

EXAMPLES:

I. <u>Sentence</u>: Coming to the city as a young man, he found a job as a newspaper reporter.

<u>Directions</u>: Substitute <u>He came</u> for <u>Coming</u>.

A. and so he found
B. and found
C. and there he had found
D and then finding
E. and had found

Your rephrased sentence will probably read: "He came to the city as a young man and found a job as a newspaper reporter." This sentence contains the correct answer: <u>B. and found</u>. A sentence which used one of the alternate phrases <u>would change the</u> meaning or <u>intention</u> of the original sentence, would be a <u>poorly written sentence</u>, or would be <u>less effective</u> than another possible revision.

II. <u>Sentence</u>: Owing to her wealth, Sarah had many suitors.

<u>Directions</u>: Begin with <u>Many men courted</u>.

A. so   B. while   C. although
D. because   E. and

4

Your rephrased sentence will probably read: "Many men courted Sarah because she was wealthy." This new sentence contains only choice D, which is the correct answer. None of the other choices will fit into an effective, correct sentence that retains the original meaning.

16. The archaeologists could only mark out the burial site,   16. ...
    for then winter came.
    Begin with Winter came before.
       A. could do nothing more   B. could not do anything
       C. could only do   D. could do something
       E. could do anything more

17. The white reader often receives some insight into the   17. ...
    reasons why black men are angry from descriptions by a
    black writer of the injustice they encounter in a white
    society.
    Begin with A black writer often gives.
       A. when describing   B. by describing
       C. he has described   D. in the descriptions
       E. because of describing

18. The agreement between the university officials and the   18. ...
    dissident students provides for student representation
    on every university committee and on the board of trustees.
    Substitute provides that for provides for.
       A. be   B. are   C. would have   D. would be   E. is to be

19. English Romanticism had its roots in German idealist   19. ...
    philosophy, first described in England by Samuel Coleridge.
    Begin with Samuel Coleridge was the first in.
       A. in which English   B. and from it English
       C. where English   D. the source of English
       E. the birth of English

20. Four months have passed since his dismissal, during which   20. ...
    time Alan has looked for work daily.
    Begin with Each day.
       A. will have passed   B. that have passed
       C. that passed   D. were to pass
       E. had passed

KEY (CORRECT ANSWERS)

1.	B	6.	B	11.	D	16.	E
2.	E	7.	B	12.	A	17.	B
3.	D	8.	A	13.	B	18.	A
4.	C	9.	C	14.	E	19.	D
5.	A	10.	E	15.	A	20.	B

English Expression

TEST

Questions 1-9.
DIRECTIONS: The following sentences contain problems in grammar, usage diction (choice of words), and idiom.

   Some sentences are correct,

   No sentence contains more than one error.
You will find that the error, if there is one, is underlined and lettered. Assume that all other elements of the sentence are correct and cannot be changed. In choosing answers, follow the requirements of standard written English. If there is an error, select the *one underlined part* that must be changed in order to make the sentence correct.
If there is no error, mark answer space E.

1. In planning your future, one must be as honest with your-   1. ...
   A   B
   self as possible, make careful decisions about the best
   course to follow to achieve a particular purpose, and,
                 C
   above all, have the courage to stand by those decisions.
                                D
   No error.
        E

2. Even though history does not actually repeat itself,   2. ...
   A
   knowledge of history can give current problems a familiar,
            B   C
   less formidable look. No error.
   D   E

3. The Curies had almost exhausted their resources, and   3. ...
                    A
   for a time it seemed unlikely that they ever would find
            B   C
   the solvent to their financial problems. No error.
           D   E

4. If the rumors are correct, Deane will not be convicted,   4. ...
   A   B
   for each of the officers on the court realizes that
   Colson and Holdman may be the real culprit and that their
                            C   D
   testimony is not completely trustworthy. No error.
                                              E

5. The citizens of Washington, like Los Angeles, prefer to   5. ...
                                A
   commute by automobile, even though motor vehicles contribute nearly as many contaminants to the air as do all other
       B   C
   sources combined. No error.
           D   E

1

6. <u>By the time Robert Vasco completes</u> his testimony, every   6. ...
             A

major executive of our company but Ray Ashurst <u>and I</u>
                                             B

<u>will have been</u> <u>accused of</u> complicity in the stock swindle.
      C   D

<u>No error.</u>
    E

7. <u>Within six months</u> the store was operating   7. ...
      A

<u>profitably and efficient</u>; shelves <u>were well stocked</u>,
         B   C

goods were selling rapidly, and the cash register
<u>was ringing constantly.</u> <u>No error.</u>
      D   E

8. Shakespeare's comedies have an advantage <u>over Shaw</u>   8. ...
                                             A

<u>in that Shakespeare's</u> were <u>written primarily</u> to entertain
          B   C

and <u>not to</u> argue for a cause. <u>No error.</u>
      D   E

9. Any true insomniac <u>is well aware of</u> the futility of   9. ...
                        A

<u>such measures as</u> drinking hot milk,
        B

<u>regular hours, deep breathing</u>, counting sheep, and
            C

<u>concentrating on</u> black velvet. <u>No error.</u>
      D   E

Questions 10-15.
DIRECTIONS: In each of the following sentences, some part of the sentence or the entire sentence is underlined. Beneath each sentence you will find five ways of phrasing the underlined part. The first of these repeats the original; the other four are different. If you think the original is better than any of the alternatives, choose answer A; otherwise choose one of the others. Select the best version and print the letter of the correct answer in the space at the right. This is a test of correctness and effectiveness of expression. In choosing answers, follow the requirements of standard written English; that is, pay attention to grammar, choice of words, sentence construction, and punctuation. Choose the answer that produces the most effective sentence - clear and exact, without awkwardness or ambiguity. Do not make a choice that changes the meaning of the original sentence.

10. The tribe of warriors believed that boys and girls should   10. ...
be <u>reared separate, and, as soon as he was weaned, the boys were taken from their mothers</u>.
    A. reared separate, and, as soon as he was weaned, the boys were taken from their mothers
    B. reared separate, and, as soon as he was weaned, a boy was taken from his mother
    C. reared separately, and, as soon as he was weaned, the boys were taken from their mothers
    D. reared separately, and, as soon as a boy was weaned, they were taken from their mothers
    E. reared separately, and, as soon as a boy was weaned, he was taken from his mother

11. <u>Despite Vesta being only the third largest, it is by</u>   11. ...
    <u>far the brightest of the known asteroids</u>.
    A. Despite Vesta being only the third largest, it is
       by far the brightest of the known asteroids.
    B. Vesta, though only the third largest asteroid, is
       by far the brightest of the known ones.
    C. Being only the third largest, yet Vesta is by far
       the brightest of the known asteroids.
    D. Vesta, though only the third largest of the known
       asteroids, is by far the brightest.
    E. Vesta is only the third largest of the asteroids,
       it being, however, the brightest one.

12. As a result of the discovery of the Dead Sea Scrolls, our   12. ...
    understanding of the roots of Christianity <u>has had to be</u>
    <u>revised considerably</u>.
    A. has had to be revised considerably
    B. have had to be revised considerably
    C. has had to undergo revision to a considerable degree
    D. have had to be subjected to considerable revision
    E. has had to be revised in a considerable way

13. Because <u>it is imminently suitable to</u> dry climates, adobe   13. ...
    has been a traditional building material throughout the
    southwestern states.
    A. it is imminently suitable to
    B. it is eminently suitable for
    C. it is eminently suitable when in
    D. of its eminent suitability with
    E. of being imminently suitable in

14. Martell is more concerned with demonstrating that racial   14. ...
    <u>prejudice exists than preventing it from doing harm, which</u>
    <u>explains</u> why his work is not always highly regarded.
    A. Martell is more concerned with demonstrating that
       racial prejudice exists than preventing it from doing
       harm, which explains
    B. Martell is more concerned with demonstrating that
       racial prejudice exists than with preventing it from
       doing harm, and this explains
    C. Martell is more concerned with demonstrating that
       racial prejudice exists than with preventing it from
       doing harm, an explanation of
    D. Martell's greater concern for demonstrating that racial
       prejudice exists than preventing it from doing harm -
       this explains
    E. Martell's greater concern for demonstrating that racial
       prejudice exists than for preventing it from doing harm
       explains

15. <u>Throughout this history of the American West there runs a</u>   15. ...
    <u>steady commentary on the deception and mistreatment of the</u>
    <u>Indians</u>.
    A. Throughout this history of the American West there runs
       a steady commentary on the deception and mistreatment of
       the Indians.
    B. There is a steady commentary provided on the deception
       and mistreatment of the Indians and it runs throughout
       this history of the American West.

3

C. The deception and mistreatment of the Indians provide a steady comment that runs throughout this history of the American West.

D. Comment on the deception and mistreatment of the Indians is steadily provided and runs throughout this history of the American West.

E. Running throughout this history of the American West is a steady commentary that is provided on the deception and mistreatment of the Indians.

Questions 16-20.

DIRECTIONS: In each of the following questions you are given a complete sentence to be rephrased according to the directions which follow it. You should rephrase the sentence mentally to save time, although you may make notes in your test book if you wish.

Below each sentence and its directions are listed words or phrases that may occur in your revised sentence. When you have thought out a good sentence, look in the choices A through E for the word or entire phrase that is included in your revised sentence, and print the letter of the correct answer in the space at the right. The word or phrase you choose should be the most accurate and most nearly complete of all the choices given, and should be part of a sentence that meets the requirements of standard written English.

Of course, a number of different sentences can be obtained if the sentence is revised according to directions, and not all of these possibilities can be included in only five choices. If you should find that you have thought of a sentence that contains none of the words or phrases listed in the choices, you should attempt to rephrase the sentence again so that it includes a word or phrase that is listed. Although the directions may at times require you to change the relationship between parts of the sentence or to make slight changes in meaning in other ways, make only those changes that the directions require; that is, keep the meaning the same, or as nearly the same as the directions permit. If you think that more than one good sentence can be made according to the directions, select the sentence that is most exact, effective, and natural in phrasing and construction.

EXAMPLES:

I. Sentence: Coming to the city as a young man, he found a job as a newspaper reporter.
   Directions: Substitute He came for Coming.
   A. and so he found
   B. and found
   C. and there he had found
   D. and then finding
   E. and had found

Your rephrased sentence will probably read: "He came to the city as a young man and found a job as a newspaper reporter." This sentence contains the correct answer: B. and found. A sentence which used one of the alternate phrases would change the meaning or intention of the original sentence, would be a poorly written sentence, or would be less effective than another possible revision.

II. Sentence: Owing to her wealth, Sarah had many suitors.
   Directions: Begin with Many men courted.
   A. so   B. while   C. although
   D. because   E. and

4

Your rephrased sentence will probably read: "Many men courted Sarah because she was wealthy." This new sentence contains only choice D, which is the correct answer. None of the other choices will fit into an effective, correct sentence that retains the original meaning.

16. The archaeologists could only mark out the burial site,   16. ...
for then winter came.
Begin with <u>Winter came before</u>.
   A. could do nothing more   B. could not do anything
   C. could only do   D. could do something
   E. could do anything more

17. The white reader often receives some insight into the   17. ...
reasons why black men are angry from descriptions by a
black writer of the injustice they encounter in a white
society.
Begin with <u>A black writer often gives</u>.
   A. when describing   B. by describing
   C. he has described   D. in the descriptions
   E. because of describing

18. The agreement between the university officials and the   18. ...
dissident students provides for student representation
on every university committee and on the board of trustees.
Substitute <u>provides that</u> for <u>provides for</u>.
   A. be B. are C. would have D. would be E. is to be

19. English Romanticism had its roots in German idealist   19. ...
philosophy, first described in England by Samuel Coleridge.
Begin with <u>Samuel Coleridge was the first in</u>.
   A. in which English   B. and from it English
   C. where English   D. the source of English
   E. the birth of English

20. Four months have passed since his dismissal, during which   20. ...
time Alan has looked for work daily.
Begin with <u>Each day</u>.
   A. will have passed   B. that have passed
   C. that passed   D. were to pass
   E. had passed

KEY (CORRECT ANSWERS)

1. B	6. B	11. D	16. E
2. E	7. B	12. A	17. B
3. D	8. A	13. B	18. A
4. C	9. C	14. E	19. D
5. A	10. E	15. A	20. B

PREPARING WRITTEN MATERIAL
EXAMINATION SECTION

DIRECTIONS FOR THIS SECTION:

Each question consists of a sentence which may or may not be an example of good English usage.

Examine each sentence, considering grammar, punctuation, spelling, capitalization, and awkwardness. Then choose the correct statement about it from the four choices below it. If the English usage in the sentence given is better than any of the changes suggested in choices B, C, or D, pick choice A. (Do not pick a choice that will change the meaning of the sentence.)

TEST 1

1. We attended a staff conference on Wednesday the new   1. ...
   safety and fire rules were discussed.
   A. This is an example of acceptable writing.
   B. The words "safety," "fire" and "rules" should begin
      with capital letters.
   C. There should be a comma after the word "Wednesday."
   D. There should be a period after the word "Wednesday"
      and the word "the" should begin with a capital letter
2. Neither the dictionary or the telephone directory could   2. ...
   be found in the office library.
   A. This is an example of acceptable writing.
   B. The word "or" should be changed to "nor."
   C. The word "library" should be spelled "libery."
   D. The word "neither" should be changed to "either."
3. The report would have been typed correctly if the typist   3. ...
   could read the draft.
   A. This is an example of acceptable writing.
   B. The word "would" should be removed.
   C. The word "have" should be inserted after the word "could."
   D. The word "correctly" should be changed to "correct."
4. The supervisor brought the reports and forms to an em-   4. ...
   employees desk.
   A. This is an example of acceptable writing.
   B. The word "brought" should be changed to "took."
   C. There should be a comma after the word "reports" and
      a comma after the word "forms."
   D. The word "employees" should be spelled "employee's."
5. It's important for all the office personnel to submit   5. ...
   their vacation schedules on time.
   A. This is an example of acceptable writing.
   B. The word "It's" should be spelled "Its."
   C. The word "their" should be spelled "they're."
   D. The word "personnel" should be spelled "personal."
6. The report, along with the accompanying documents, were   6. ...
   submitted for review.
   A. This is an example of acceptable writing.
   B. The words "were submitted" should be changed to "was
      submitted."
   C. The word "accompanying" should be spelled "accompaning."
   D. The comma after the word "report" should be taken out.
7. If others must use your files, be certain that they   7. ...
   understand how the system works, but insist that you do
   all the filing and refiling.
   A. This is an example of acceptable writing.

1

   B. There should be a period after the word "works," and the
      word "but" should start a new sentence
   C. The words "filing" and "refiling" should be spelled
      "fileing" and "refileing."
   D. There should be a comma after the word "but."
8. The appeal was not considered because of its late   8. ...
   arrival.
   A. This is an example of acceptable writing.
   B. The word "its" should be changed to "it's."
   C. The word "its" should be changed to "the."
   D. The words "late arrival" should be changed to
      "arrival late."
9. The letter must be read carefuly to determine under which   9. ...
   subject it should be filed.
   A. This is an example of acceptable writing.
   B. The word "under" should be changed to "at."
   C. The word "determine" should be spelled "determin."
   D. The word "carefuly" should be spelled "carefully."
10. He showed potential as an office manager, but he lacked   10. ...
    skill in delegating work.
    A. This is an example of acceptable writing.
    B. The word "delegating" should be spelled "delagating."
    C. The word "potential" should be spelled "potencial."
    D. The words "he lacked" should be changed to "was lacking."

TEST 2

1. The supervisor wants that all staff members report to   1. ...
   the office at 9:00 A.M.
   A. This is an example of acceptable writing.
   B. The word "that" should be removed and the word "to"
      should be inserted after the word "members."
   C. There should be a comma after the word "wants" and a
      comma after the word "office."
   D. The word "wants" should be changed to "want" and the
      word "shall" should be inserted after the word "members."
2. Every morning the clerk opens the office mail and   2. ...
   distributes it.
   A. This is an example of acceptable writing.
   B. The word "opens" should be changed to "open."
   C. The word "mail" should be changed to "letters."
   D. The word "it" should be changed to "them."
3. The secretary typed more fast on an electric typewriter   3. ...
   than on a manual typewriter.
   A. This is an example of acceptable writing.
   B. The words "more fast" should be changed to "faster."
   C. There should be a comma after the words "electric
      typewriter."
   D. The word "than" should be changed to "then."
4. The new stenographer needed a desk a typewriter, a chair   4. ...
   and a blotter.
   A. This is an example of acceptable writing.
   B. The word "blotter" should be spelled "blodder."
   C. The word "stenographer" should begin with a capital letter.
   D. There should be a comma after the word "desk."

2

5. The recruiting officer said, "There are many different   5. ...
   goverment jobs available."
   A. This is an example of acceptable writing.
   B. The word "There" should not be capitalized.
   C. The word "goverment" should be spelled "government."
   D. The comma after the word "said" should be removed.
6. He can recommend a mechanic whose work is reliable.   6. ...
   A. This is an example of acceptable writing.
   B. The word "reliable" should be spelled "relyable."
   C. The word "whose" should be spelled "who's."
   D. The word "mechanic" should be spelled "mecanic."
7. She typed quickly; like someone who had not a moment to   7. ...
   lose.
   A. This is an example of acceptable writing.
   B. The word "not" should be removed.
   C. The semicolon should be changed to a comma.
   D. The word "quickly" should be placed before instead of
      after the word "typed."
8. She insisted that she had to much work to do.   8. ...
   A. This is an example of acceptable writing.
   B. The word "insisted" should be spelled "incisted."
   C. The word "to" used in front of "much" should be spelled
      "too."
   D. The word "do" should be changed to "be done."
9. He excepted praise from his supervisor for a job well done. 9. ...
   A. This is an example of acceptable writing.
   B. The word "excepted" should be spelled "accepted."
   C. The order of the words "well done" should be changed
      to "done well."
   D. There should be a comma after the word "supervisor."
10. What appears to be intentional errors in grammar occur   10. ...
    several times in the passage.
    A. This is an example of acceptable writing.
    B. The word "occur" should be spelled "occurr."
    C. The word "appears" should be changed to "appear."
    D. The phrase "several times" should be changed to "from
       time to time."

TEST 3

Questions 1-5.
DIRECTIONS: Same as for Tests 1 and 2.
1. The clerk could have completed the assignment on time   1. ...
   if he knows where these materials were located.
   A. This is an example of acceptable writing.
   B. The word "knows" should be replaced by "had known."
   C. The word "were" should be replaced by "had been."
   D. The words "where these materials were located" should
      be replaced by "the location of these materials."
2. All employees should be given safety training. Not just   2. ...
   those who have accidents.
   A. This is an example of acceptable writing.
   B. The period after the word "training" should be changed
      to a colon.

3

    C. The period after the word "training" should be changed
       to a semicolon, and the first letter of the word "Not"
       should be changed to a small "n."
    D. The period after the word "training" should be changed
       to a comma, and the first letter of the word "Not"
       should be changed to a small "n."

3. This proposal is designed to promote employee awareness   3. ...
   of the suggestion program, to encourage employee participation in the program, and to increase the number of suggestions submitted.
    A. This is an example of acceptable writing.
    B. The word "proposal" should be spelled "preposal."
    C. The words "to increase the number of suggestions
       submitted" should be changed to "an increase in the
       number of suggestions is expected."
    D. The word "promote" should be changed to "enhance" and
       the word "increase" should be changed to "add to."

4. The introduction of inovative managerial techniques   4. ...
   should be preceded by careful analysis of the specific
   circumstances and conditions in each department.
    A. This is an example of acceptable writing.
    B. The word "techniques" should be spelled "techneques."
    C. The word "inovative" should be spelled "innovative."
    D. A comma should be placed after the word "circumstances"
       and after the word "conditions."

5. This occurrence indicates that such criticism embarrasses 5. ...
   him.
    A. This is an example of acceptable writing.
    B. The word "occurrence" should be spelled "occurence."
    C. The word "criticism" should be spelled "critisism."
    D. The word "embarrasses" should be spelled "embarasses."

KEY (CORRECT ANSWERS)

TEST 1	TEST 2	TEST 3
1. D	1. B	1. B
2. B	2. A	2. D
3. C	3. B	3. A
4. D	4. D	4. C
5. A	5. C	5. A
6. B	6. A	
7. A	7. C	
8. A	8. C	
9. D	9. B	
10. A	10. C	

EXAMINATION SECTION

TEST 1

DIRECTIONS: Each question or incomplete statement is followed by several suggested answers or completions. Select the one that BEST answers the question or completes the statement. *PRINT THE LETTER OF THE CORRECT ANSWER IN THE SPACE AT THE RIGHT.*

1. The one of the following which is the CHIEF reason for the difference between the administration of justice agencies and that of other units in public administration is that
   A. correctional institutions are concerned with security
   B. some defendants are proven to be innocent after trial
   C. the administration of justice is much more complicated than other aspects of public administration
   D. correctional institutions produce services their "clients" or "customers" fail to understand or ask for

1.___

2. Of the following, the MOST important reason why employees resist change is that
   A. they have not received adequate training in preparation for the change
   B. experience has shown that when new ideas don't work, employees get blamed and not the individuals responsible for the new ideas
   C. new ideas and methods almost always represent a threat to the security of the individuals involved
   D. new ideas often are not practical and disrupt operations unnecessarily

2.___

3. Stress situations are ideal for building up a backlog of knowledge about an employee's behavior. Not only does it inform the supervisor of many aspects of a person's behavior patterns, but it is also vitally important to have fore-knowledge of how people behave under stress.
   The one of the following which is NOT implied by this passage is that
   A. a person under stress may give some indication of his unsuitability for work in an institution
   B. putting people under stress is the best means of determining their usual patterns of behavior
   C. stress situations may give important clues about performance in the service
   D. there is a need to know about a person's reaction to situations "when the chips are down"

3.___

4. There are situations requiring a supervisor to give direct orders to subordinates assigned to work under the direct control of other supervisors.
   Under which of the following conditions would this shift of command responsibility be MOST appropriate?
   A. Emergency operations require the cooperative action of two or more organizational units.

4.___

B. One of the other supervisors is not doing his job,
thus defeating the goals of the organization.

C. The subordinates are performing their assigned tasks
in the absence of their own supervisor.

D. The subordinates ask a superior officer who is not
their own supervisor how to perform an assignment
given them by their supervisor.

5. The one of the following which BEST differentiates staff   5.___
supervision from line supervision is that
   A. staff supervision has the authority to immediately
     correct a line subordinate's action
   B. staff supervision is an advisory relationship
   C. line supervision goes beyond the normal boundaries
     of direct supervision within a "command"
   D. line supervision does not report findings and make
     recommendations

6. Decision-making is a rational process calling for a   6.___
"suspended judgment" by the supervisor until all the facts
have been ascertained and analyzed, and the consequences
of alternative courses of action studied; *then* the
decision maker
   A. acts as both judge and jury and selects what he believes
     to be the best of the alternative plans
   B. consults with those who will be most directly involved
     to obtain a recommendation as to the most appropriate
     course of action
   C. reviews the facts which he has already analyzed,
     reduces his thoughts to writing, and selects that
     course of action which can have the fewest negative
     consequences if his thinking contains an error
   D. stops, considers the matter for at least a 24-hour
     period, before referring it to a superior for
     evaluation

7. Decision-making can be defined as the   7.___
   A. delegation of authority and responsibility to persons
     capable of performing their assigned duties with
     moderate or little supervision
   B. imposition of a supervisor's decision upon a work
     group
   C. technique of selecting the course of action with the
     most desired consequences, and the least undesired
     or unexpected consequences
   D. process principally concerned with improvement of
     procedures

8. A supervisor who is not well-motivated and has no desire   8.___
to accept basic responsibilities will
   A. compromise to the extent of permitting poor performance
     for lengthy periods without correction
   B. get good performance from his work group if the
     employees are satisfied with their pay and other
     working conditions
   C. not have marginal workers in his work group if the
     work is interesting
   D. perform adequately as long as the work of his group
     consists of routine operations

9. A supervisor is more than a bond or connecting link   9.___
    between two levels of employees. He has joint responsibility
    which must be shared with both management and with the
    work group.
    Of the following, the item which BEST expresses the meaning
    of this statement is:
    A. A supervisor works with both management and the work
       group and must reconcile the differences between them.
    B. In management, the supervisor is solely concerned with
       efforts directing the work of his subordinates.
    C. The supervisory role is basically that of a liaison
       man between management and the work force.
    D. What a supervisor says and does when confronted with
       day-to-day problems depends upon his level in the
       organization.

10. Operations research is the observation of operations in   10.___
    business or government, and it utilizes both hypotheses
    and controlled experiments to determine the outcome of
    decisions. In effect, it reproduces the future impact on
    the decision in a clinical environment suited to intensive
    study.
    Operations research has
    A. been more promising than applied research in the
       ascertaining of knowledge for the purpose of
       decision-making
    B. never been amenable to fact analysis on the grand
       scale
    C. not been used extensively in government
    D. proven to be the only rational and logical approach
       to decision-making on long-range problems

11. Assume that a civilian makes a complaint regarding the   11.___
    behavior of a certain worker to the supervisor of the
    worker. The supervisor regards the complaint as
    unjustified and unreasonable.
    In these circumstances, the supervisor
    A. must make a written note of the complaint and forward
       it through channels to the unit or individual
       responsible for complaint investigations
    B. should assure the complainant that disciplinary
       action will be appropriate to the seriousness of the
       alleged offense
    C. should immediately summon the worker if he is
       available so that the latter may attempt to straighten
       out the difficulty
    D. should inform the complainant that his complaint
       appears to be unjustified and unreasonable

12. Modern management usually establishes a personal history   12.___
    folder for an employee at the time of hiring. Disciplinary
    matters appear in such personal history folders. Employees
    do not like the idea of disciplinary actions appearing in
    their permanent personal folders.
    Authorities believe that

    A. after a few years have passed since the commission
       of the infraction, disciplinary actions should be
       removed from folders
    B. disciplinary actions should remain in folders; it is
       not the records but the use of records that requires
       detailed study
    C. most personnel have not had disciplinary action taken
       against them and would resent the removal of
       disciplinary actions from such folders
    D. there is no point in removing disciplinary actions
       from personal history folders since employees who
       have been guilty of infractions should not be allowed
       to forget their infractions

13. While supervisors should not fear the acceptance of   13.___
    responsibility, they
    A. generally seek out responsibility that subordinates
       should exercise, particularly when the supervisors
       do not have sufficient work to do
    B. must be on guard against the abuse of authority that
       often accompanies the acceptance of total responsibility
    C. should avoid responsibility that is customarily
       exercised by their superiors
    D. who are anxious for promotions accept responsibility
       but do not exercise the authority warranted by the
       responsibility

14. Planning is part of the decision-making process. By   14.___
    planning is meant the development of details of alternative
    plans of action.
    The key to *effective* planning is
    A. careful research to determine whether a tentative
       plan has been tried at some time in the past
    B. participation by employees in planning, preferably
       those employees who will be involved in putting
       the selected plan into action
    C. speed; poor plans can be discarded after they are
       put into effect while good plans usually are not
       put into effect because of delays
    D. writing the plan up in considerable detail and then
       forwarding the plan, through channels, to the executive
       officer having final approval of the plan

15. Equating strict discipline with punitive measures and lax   15.___
    discipline with rehabilitation creates a false dichotomy.
    The one of the statements given below that would BEST
    follow from the belief expressed in this statement is
    that discipline
    A. is important for treatment
    B. militates against treatment programs
    C. is not an important consideration in institutions
       where effective rehabilitation programs prevail
    D. minimizes the need for punitive measures if it is
       strict

16. If training starts at the lower level of command, it is like planting a seed in tilled ground but removing the sun and rain. Seeds cannot grow unless they have help from above.
    Of the following, the MOST appropriate conclusion to be drawn from this statement is that
    A. the head of an institution may not delegate authority for the planning of an institutional training program for staff
    B. on-the-job training is better than formalized training courses
    C. regularly scheduled training courses must be planned in advance
    D. staff training is the responsibility of higher levels of command

16.___

17. The one of the following that BEST describes the meaning of "in-service staff training" is:
    A. The training of personnel who are below average in performance
    B. The training given to each employee throughout his employment
    C. The training of staff only in their own specialized fields
    D. Classroom training where the instructor and employees develop a positive and productive relationship leading to improved efficiency on the job

17.___

18. All bureau personnel should be concerned about, and involved in, public relations.
    Of the following, the MOST important reason for this statement is that
    A. an institution is an agency of the government supported by public funds and responsible to the public
    B. institutions are places of public business and, therefore, the public is interested in them
    C. some personnel need publicity in order to advance
    D. personnel sometimes need publicity in order to ensure that their grievances are acted upon by higher authority

18.___

19. The MOST important factor in establishing a disciplinary policy in an organization is
    A. consistency of application
    B. strict supervisors
    C. strong enforcement
    D. the degree of toughness or laxity

19.___

20. The FIRST step in planning a program is to
    A. clearly define the objectives
    B. estimate the costs
    C. hire a program director
    D. solicit funds

20.___

21. The PRIMARY purpose of control in an organization is to
    A. punish those who do not do their job well
    B. get people to do what is necessary to achieve an objective
    C. develop clearly stated rules and regulations
    D. regulate expenditures

21.___

22. The UNDERLYING principle of *sound* administration is to   22.___
    A. base administration on investigation of facts
    B. have plenty of resources available
    C. hire a strong administrator
    D. establish a broad policy

23. An IMPORTANT aspect to keep in mind during the decision-   23.___
    making process is that
    A. all possible alternatives for attaining goals should
       be sought out and considered
    B. considering various alternatives only leads to
       confusion
    C. once a decision has been made, it cannot be retracted
    D. there is only one correct method to reach any goal

24. Implementation of accountability requires   24.___
    A. a leader who will not hesitate to take punitive action
    B. an established system of communication from the
       bottom to the top
    C. explicit directives from leaders
    D. too much expense to justify it

25. The CHIEF danger of a decentralized control system is that   25.___
    A. excessive reports and communications will be generated
    B. problem areas may not be detected readily
    C. the expense will become prohibitive
    D. this will result in too many "chiefs"

KEY (CORRECT ANSWERS)

1. D		11. D
2. C		12. A
3. B		13. B
4. A		14. B
5. B		15. A
6. A		16. D
7. C		17. B
8. A		18. A
9. A		19. A
10. C		20. A

21. B
22. A
23. A
24. B
25. B

TEST 2

DIRECTIONS: Each question or incomplete statement is followed by several suggested answers or completions. Select the one that BEST answers the question or completes the statement. *PRINT THE LETTER OF THE CORRECT ANSWER IN THE SPACE AT THE RIGHT.*

1. When giving orders to his subordinates, a certain supervisor often includes information as to why the work is necessary.
   This approach by the supervisor is *generally*
   A. *inadvisable*, since it appears that he is avoiding responsibility and wishes to blame his superiors
   B. *inadvisable*, since it creates the impression that he is trying to impress the subordinates with his importance
   C. *advisable*, since it serves to motivate the subordinates by giving them a reason for wanting to do the work
   D. *advisable*, since it shows that he is knowledgeable and is in control of his assignments

2. Some supervisors often ask capable, professional subordinates to get some work done with questions such as: "Mary, would you try to complete that work today?"
   The use of such request orders *usually*
   A. gets results which are as good as or better than results from direct orders
   B. shows the supervisor to be weak and lowers the respect of his subordinates
   C. provokes resentment as compared to the use of direct orders
   D. leads to confusion as to the proper procedure to follow when carrying out orders

3. Assume that a supervisor, because of an emergency when time was essential, and in the absence of his immediate superior, went out of the chain of command to get a decision from a higher level.
   It would consequently be MOST appropriate for the immediate superior to
   A. reprimand him for his action, since the long-range consequences are far more detrimental than the immediate gain
   B. encourage him to use this method, since the chain of command is an outmoded and discredited system which inhibits productive work
   C. order him to refrain from any repetition of this action in the future
   D. support him as long as he informed the superior of the action at the earliest opportunity

1.____

2.____

3.____

7

4. A supervisor gave instructions which he knew were somewhat   4.__
   complex to a subordinate. He then asked the subordinate
   to repeat the instructions to him.
   The supervisor's decision to have the subordinate repeat
   the instructions was
      A. *good practice*, mainly because the subordinate would
         realize the importance of carefully following
         instructions
      B. *poor practice*, mainly because the supervisor should
         have given the employee time to ponder the instructions,
         and then, if necessary, to ask questions
      C. *good practice*, mainly because the supervisor could
         see whether the subordinate had any apparent problem
         in understanding the instructions
      D. *poor practice*, mainly because the subordinate should
         not be expected to have the same degree of knowledge
         as the supervisor

5. Supervisors and subordinates must successfully communicate   5.__
   with each other in order to work well together.
   Which of the following statements concerning communication
   of this type is CORRECT?
      A. When speaking to his subordinates, a supervisor should
         make every effort to appear knowledgeable about all
         aspects of their work.
      B. Written communications should be prepared by the
         supervisor at his own level of comprehension.
      C. The average employee tends to give meaning to communi-
         cation according to his personal interpretation.
      D. The effective supervisor communicates as much informa-
         tion as he has available to anyone who is interested.

6. A supervisor should be aware of situations in which it   6.__
   is helpful to put his orders to his subordinates in
   writing.
   Which of the following situations would MOST likely call
   for a WRITTEN order rather than an ORAL order? The order
      A. gives complicated instructions which vary from
         ordinary practice
      B. involves the performance of duties for which the
         subordinate is responsible
      C. directs subordinates to perform duties similar to
         those which they performed in the recent past
      D. concerns a matter that must be promptly completed
         or dealt with

7. Assume that a supervisor discovers that a false rumor   7.__
   about possible layoffs has spread among his subordinates
   through the grapevine.
   Of the following, the BEST way for the supervisor to
   deal with this situation is to
      A. use the grapevine to leak accurate information
      B. call a meeting to provide information and to answer
         questions
      C. post a notice on the bulletin board denying the rumor
      D. institute procedures designed to eliminate the
         grapevine

8. Communications in an organization with many levels becomes   8.___
subject to different interpretations at each level and
have a tendency to become distorted. The more levels there
are in an organization, the greater the likelihood that the
final recipient of a communication will get the wrong
message.
The one of the following statements which BEST supports
the foregoing viewpoint is:
   A. Substantial communications problems exist at high
      management levels in organizations.
   B. There is a relationship in an organization between
      the number of hierarchical levels and interference
      with communications.
   C. An opportunity should be given to subordinates at all
      levels to communicate their views with impunity.
   D. In larger organizations, there tends to be more inter-
      ference with downward communications than with upward
      communications.

9. A subordinate comes to you, his supervisor, to ask a   9.___
detailed question about a new agency directive; however,
you do not know the answer.
Of the following, the MOST helpful response to give the
subordinate is to
   A. point out that since your own supervisor has failed
      to keep you informed of this matter, it is probably
      unimportant
   B. give the most logical interpretation you can, based
      on your best judgment
   C. ask him to raise the question with other supervisors
      until he finds one who knows the answer, then let you
      know also
   D. explain that you do not know and assure him that you
      will get the information for him

10. The traditional view of management theory is that communi-   10.___
cation in an organization should follow the table of
organization. A newer theory holds that timely communication
often requires bypassing certain steps in the hierarchical
chain.
However, the MAIN advantage of using formal channels of
communication within an organization is that
   A. an employee is thereby restricted in his relationships
      to his immediate superior and his immediate subordinates
   B. information is thereby transmitted to everyone who
      should be informed
   C. the organization will have an appeal channel, or a
      mechanism by which subordinates can go over their
      superior's head
   D. employees are thereby encouraged to exercise individual
      initiative

11. It is unfair to hold subordinates responsible for the   11.___
performance of duties for which they do not have the
requisite authority.
When this is done, it violates the principle that

    A. responsibility *cannot be greater* than that implied
       by delegated authority
    B. responsibility *should be greater* than that implied
       by delegated authority
    C. authority *cannot be greater* than that implied by
       delegated responsibility
    D. authority *should be greater* than that implied by
       delegated responsibility

12. Assume that a supervisor wishes to delegate some tasks to   12.__
    a capable subordinate.
    It would be MOST in keeping with the principles of
    delegation for the supervisor to
    A. ask another supervisor who is experienced in the
       delegated tasks to evaluate the subordinate's work
       from time to time
    B. monitor continually the subordinate's performance by
       carefully reviewing his work at every step
    C. request experienced employees to submit peer ratings
       of the work of the subordinate
    D. tell the subordinates what problems are likely to be
       encountered and specify which problems to report on

13. There are *three* types of leadership: *autocratic*, in   13.__
    which the leader makes the decisions and seeks compliance
    from his subordinates; *democratic*, in which the leader
    consults with his subordinates and lets them help set
    policy; and *free rein*, in which the leader acts as an
    information center and exercises minimum control over his
    subordinates.
    A supervisor can be MOST effective if he decides to
    A. use democratic leadership techniques exclusively
    B. avoid the use of autocratic leadership techniques
       entirely
    C. employ the three types of leadership according to
       the situation
    D. rely mainly on autocratic leadership techniques

14. During a busy period of work, Employee A asked his super-   14.__
    visor for leave in order to take an ordinary vacation.
    The supervisor denied the request. The following day,
    Employee B asked for leave during the same period because
    his wife had just gone to the hospital for an indeterminate
    stay and he had family matters to tend to.
    Of the following, the BEST way for the supervisor to deal
    with Employee B's request is to
    A. grant the request and give the reason to the other
       employee
    B. suggest that the employee make his request to higher
       management
    C. delay the request immediately since granting it would
       show favoritism
    D. defer any decision until the duration of the hospital
       stay is determined

15. Assume that you are a supervisor and that a subordinate   15.___
    tells you he has a grievance.
    In general, you should FIRST
       A. move the grievance forward in order to get a prompt
          decision
       B. discourage this type of behavior on the part of
          subordinates
       C. attempt to settle the grievance
       D. refer the subordinate to the personnel office

16. A supervisor may have available a large variety of rewards   16.___
    he can use to motivate his subordinates. However, some
    supervisors choose the wrong rewards.
    A supervisor is *most likely* to make such a mistake if he
       A. appeals to a subordinate's desire to be well-regarded
          by his co-workers
       B. assumes that the subordinate's goals and preferences
          are the same as his own
       C. conducts in-depth discussions with a subordinate in
          order to discover his preference
       D. limits incentives to those rewards which he is
          authorized to provide or to recommend

17. Employee performance appraisal is open to many kinds of   17.___
    errors.
    When a supervisor is preparing such an appraisal, he is
    most likely to commit an error if
       A. employees are indifferent to the consequences of
          their performance appraisals
       B. the entire period for which the evaluation is being
          made is taken into consideration
       C. standard measurement criteria are used as performance
          benchmarks
       D. personal characteristics of employees which are not
          job-related are given weight

18. Assume that a supervisor finds that a report prepared by   18.___
    an employee is unsatisfactory and should be done over.
    Which of the following should the supervisor do?
       A. Give the report to another employee who can
          complete it properly.
       B. Have the report done over by the same employee after
          successfully training him.
       C. Hold a meeting to train all the employees so as not
          to single out the employee who performed unsatisfactorily
       D. Accept the report so as not to discourage the employee
          and then make the corrections himself.

19. Employees sometimes wish to have personal advice and   19.___
    counseling, in confidence, about their job-related problems.
    These problems may include such concerns as health matters,
    family difficulties, alcoholism, debts, emotional dis-
    turbances, etc.
    Such assistance is BEST provided through
       A. maintenance of an exit interview program to find
          reasons for, and solutions to, turnover problems

B. arrangements for employees to discuss individual problems informally outside normal administrative channels
C. procedures which allow employees to submit anonymous inquiries to the personnel department
D. special hearing committees consisting of top management in addition to immediate supervisors

20. An employee is always a member of some unit of the formal organization. He may also be a member of an informal work group.
With respect to employee productivity and job satisfaction, the informal work group can MOST accurately be said to
   A. have no influence of any kind on its members
   B. influence its members negatively only
   C. influence its members positively only
   D. influence its members negatively or positively

20.___

21. In order to encourage employees to make suggestions, many public agencies have employee suggestion programs.
What is the MAJOR benefit of such a program to the agency as a whole? It
   A. brings existing or future problems to management's attention
   B. reduces the number of minor accidents
   C. requires employees to share in decision-making responsibilities
   D. reveals employees who have inadequate job knowledge

21.___

22. Assume that you have been asked to interview a seemingly shy applicant for a temporary position in your department.
For you to ask the kinds of questions that begin with "What," "Where," "Why," "When," "Who," and "How," is
   A. *good practice*; it informs the applicant that he must conform to the requirements of the department
   B. *poor practice*; it exceeds the extent and purpose of an initial interview
   C. *good practice*; it encourages the applicant to talk to a greater extent
   D. *poor practice*; it encourages the applicant to dominate the discussion

22.___

23. In recent years, job enlargement or job enrichment has tended to replace job simplification.
Those who advocate job enrichment or enlargement consider it *desirable* CHIEFLY because
   A. it allows supervisors to control closely the activities of subordinates
   B. it produces greater job satisfaction through reduction of responsibility
   C. most employees prefer to avoid work which is new and challenging
   D. positions with routinized duties are unlikely to provide job satisfaction

23.___

24. Job rotation is a training method in which an employee   24.___
    temporarily changes places with another employee of
    equal rank.
    What is usually the MAIN purpose of job rotation? To
       A. politely remove the person being rotated from an
          unsuitable assignment
       B. increase skills and provide broader experience
       C. prepare the person being rotated for a permanent
          change
       D. test the skills of the person being rotated

25. There are several principles that a supervisor needs to   25.___
    know if he is to deal adequately with his training
    responsibilities.
    Which of the following is usually NOT a principle of
    training?
       A. People should be trained according to their individual
          needs.
       B. People can learn by being told or shown how to do
          work, but best of all by doing work under guidance.
       C. People can be easily trained even if they have no
          desire to learn.
       D. Training should be planned, scheduled, executed, and
          evaluated systematically.

KEY (CORRECT ANSWERS)

1. C		11. A	
2. A		12. D	
3. D		13. C	
4. C		14. A	
5. C		15. C	
6. A		16. B	
7. B		17. D	
8. B		18. B	
9. D		19. B	
10. B		20. D	

21. A
22. C
23. D
24. B
25. C

BASIC FUNDAMENTALS OF
WRITTEN COMMUNICATION

CONTENTS

BASIC FUNDAMENTALS OF
WRITTEN COMMUNICATION

INSTRUCTIONAL
OBJECTIVES

1. Ability to write legibly.

2. Ability to fill out forms and applications correctly.

3. Ability to take messages and notes accurately.

4. Ability to write letters effectively.

5. Ability to write directions and instructions clearly.

6. Ability to outline written and spoken information.

7. Ability to persuade or teach others through written communication.

8. Ability to write effective overviews and summaries.

9. Ability to make smooth transitions within written communications.

10. Ability to use language forms appropriate for the reader.

11. Ability to prepare effective informational reports.

CONTENT

INTRODUCTION

Public-service employees are required to prepare written communications for a variety of purposes. Written communication is a fundamental tool, not only for the public-service occupations, but throughout the world of work. Many public-service occupations require written communication with ordinary citizens of diverse backgrounds, so the trainee should develop the ability to write in simple, nontechnical language that the ordinary citizen will understand.

This unit is designed to develop the student's ability to communicate effectively in writing for a number of different purposes and in a number of different formats. Whatever the particular purpose or format, however, effective writing will require the writer:

° to have a clear idea of his purpose and his audience;

° to organize his thoughts and information in an orderly way;

° to express himself concisely, accurately, and concretely;

° to report relevant facts;

° to explain and summarize ideas clearly; and

° to evaluate the effectiveness of his communication.

1. BUSINESS WRITING

Several forms of written communication tend to recur frequently in most public-service agencies, including:

° letters

° forms

° memoranda

° minutes of meetings

° short reports

° telegrams and cables

° news releases

° and many others

The public-service employee should be familiar with the principles of writing in these forms, and should be able to apply them in preparing effective communications.

Letters

Every letter sent from a public-service agency should be considered an ambassador of goodwill. The impression it creates may mean the difference between favorable public attitudes or unfavorable ones. It may mean the difference between creating a friend or an enemy for the agency. Every public-service employee has a responsibility to serve the public effectively and to provide services in an efficient and courteous manner. The letters an agency sends out reflect its attitudes toward the public.

The impression a letter creates depends upon both its appearance and its tone. A letter which shows erasures and pen written corrections gives an impression that the sending agency is slovenly. Similarly, a rude or impersonal letter creates the impression that the agency is insensitive or unfeeling. In preparing letters, the employee should apply principles of

style and tone which will serve to create the most favorable
impression.

Select the Letter Type. The two most common types of business
letters are letters of inquiry and letters of response - that
is, "asking" letters and "answering" letters. Whichever type
of letter the employee is asked to write, the following guidelines will simplify the task and help to achieve a style and
tone which will create a favorable impression on the reader.

Select the Right Format. Several styles of letter format are
in common use today, including:

- the indented format,
- the block format, and
- the semi-block format.

Modified forms of these are also in use in some offices. The
student should become familiar with the formats preferred for
usage in his office, and be able to use whichever form the
employer requests.

Know the Letter Elements. Every letter includes certain basic
elements, such as:

- the letterhead, which identifies the name and address of
  the sender.
- the date on which the letter was transmitted.
- the inside address, with the name, street, city, and state
  of the addressee.
- the salutation, greeting the addressee.
- the body, containing the message.
- the complimentary close, the "good-bye" of the business
  letter.
- the signature, handwritten by the sender.
- the typed signature, the typewritten name and title of the
  sender.

In addition, several other elements are occasionally found in
business letters:

- the *attention line*, directing the letter to the attention
  of a particular individual or his representative.
- the *subject line*, informing the reader at a glance of the
  subject of the letter.

3

° the *enclosure notation*, noting items enclosed with the letter.

° the *carbon-copy notation*, listing other persons who receive copies of the letter.

° the *postscript*, an afterthought sometimes (but not normally) added following the last typed line of the letter.

Be Brief. Use only the words which help to say what is needed in a clear and straightforward manner. Do not repeat information already known to the reader, or contained elsewhere in the letter. Likewise, do not repeat information contained in the letter being answered. Rather than repeat the content of a previous letter, one can say something like, "Please refer to our letter dated March 5."

An employee can shorten his letters by using single words that serve the same function as longer phrases. Many commonly used phrases can be replaced by single words. For example,

Phrase	Single word
in order to	to
in reference to	about
in the amount of	for, of
in a number of cases	some
in view of	because
with regard to	about, in

Similarly, avoid the use of adjectives and nouns that are formed from verbs. If the root verbs are used instead, the writing will be more concise and more vivid. For example,

Noun form	Verb form
We made an adjustment on our books	We adjusted our books
We are sorry we cannot make a replacement of	We are sorry we cannot replace
Please make a correction in our order	Please correct our order

Be on the lookout for unnecessary adjectives and adverbs which tend to clutter letters without adding information or improving style. Such unnecessary words tend to distract the reader and make it more difficult for him to grasp the main points. Observe how the superfluous words, italicized in the following example, obscure the meaning: "You may be *very much* disappointed to learn that the *excessively large* demand for our *highly popular recent* publication, 'Your Income Taxes,' has led to an *unexpected* shortage of this *attractive* publication and we *sadly* expect they will not be replenished until *quite* late this year."

Summarizing, then, *a good letter is simple and clear, with short, simple words, sentences, and paragraphs. Related parts of sentences and paragraphs are kept together and placed in an order which makes it easy for the reader to follow the main thoughts.*

Be Natural. Whenever possible, use a human touch. Use names and personal pronouns to let the reader know the letter was written by a person, not an institution. Instead of saying, "It is the policy of this agency to contact its clients once each year to confirm their status," try this: "Our policy, Mr. Jones, is to confirm your status once each year."

Use Concrete Nouns. Avoid using abstract words and generalizations. Use names of objects, places, and persons rather than abstractions.

Use Active Verbs. The passive voice gives a motionless, weak tone to most writing. Instead of "The minutes were taken by Mrs. Smith," say, "Mrs. Smith took the minutes." Instead of "The plans were prepared by the banquet committee," say, "The banquet committee prepared the plans."

Use a Natural Tone. Many people tend to become hard, cold, and unnatural the moment they write a letter. *Communicating by letter should have the same natural tone of conversation used in everyday speech.* One way to achieve a natural and personal tone in the majority of letters is through the use of personal pronouns. Instead of saying, "Referring to your letter of March 5, reporting the non-receipt of goods ordered last February 15, please be advised that the goods were shipped as requested," say, "I am sorry to hear that you failed to receive the items you ordered last February 15. We shipped them the same day we received your letter."

Forms

In most businesses and public service agencies, repetitive work is simplified by the use of *forms*. Forms exist for nearly every purpose imaginable: for ordering supplies, preparing invoices, applying for jobs, applying for insurance, paying taxes, recording inventories, and so on.

While the forms encountered in different agencies may differ widely, several principles should be applied in completing any form:

° *Legibility*. Entries on forms should be clear and legible. Print or type wherever possible. When space provided is insufficient, attach a supplementary sheet to the form.

° *Completeness*. Make an entry in every space provided on the form. If a particular space does not apply to the applicant, enter there the term "N/A" (for "not applicable"). The reader of the completed form will then know that the applicant did not simply overlook that space.

° *Conciseness*. Forms are intended to elicit a maximum amount of information in the least possible space. When completing a form, it is usually not necessary to write complete sentences. Provide the necessary information in the least possible words.

° *Accuracy*. Be sure the information provided on the form is accurate. If the entry is a number, such as a social security number or an address, double-check the correctness of the number. Be sure of the spelling of names, No one appreciates receiving a communication in which his name is misspelled.

Memoranda

The written communications passing between offices or departments are usually transmitted in a form known as *"interoffice memorandum."* The headings most often used on such "memos" are:

° TO: identifying the addressee,
° FROM: identifying the sender or the originating office,
° SUBJECT: identifying briefly the subject of the memo,
° DATE: identifying the date the memo was prepared.

Larger agencies may also use headings such as FILE or REFERENCE NO. to aid in filing and retrieving memoranda.

In writing a memo, many of the same rules for letter-writing may be applied. Both the appearance and tone of the memo should create a pleasing impression. The format should be neat and follow the standards set by the originating office. The tone should be friendly, courteous, and considerate. The language should be clear, concise, and complete.

Memos usually dispense with salutations, complimentary closings, and signatures of the writers. In most other respects, however, the memorandum will follow the rules of good letter-writing.

Minutes of Meetings

Most formal public-service organization conduct meetings from time to time at which group decisions are made about agency policies, procedures, and work assignments. The records of such meetings are called *minutes*.

Minutes should be written as clearly and simply as possible, summarizing only the essential facts and decisions made at the meeting. While some issue may have been discussed at great length, only the final decision or resolution made of it should be recorded in the minutes. Information of this sort is usually included:

° Time and place of the call to order,

° Presiding officer and secretary,

° Voting members present (with names, if a small organization),

° Approval and corrections of previous minutes,

° Urgent business,

° Old business,

° New business,

° Time of adjournment,

° Signature of recorder.

Minutes should be written in a factual and objective style. The opinions of the recorder should not be in evidence. Every item of business coming up before a meeting should be included in the minutes, together with its disposition. For example:

° "M/S/P (Moved, seconded, passed) that Mr. Thomas Jones take responsibility for rewriting the personnel procedures manual."

° "Discussion of the summer vacation schedule was tabled until the next meeting."

° "M/S/P, a resolution that no client of the agency should be kept waiting more than 20 minutes for an interview."

Note that considerable discussion may have surrounded each of the above items in the minutes, but that only the topic and its resolution are recorded.

7

Short Reports

The public-service employee often is called upon to prepare a short report gathering and interpreting information on a single topic. Reports of this kind are sometimes prepared so that all the relevant information may be assembled in one place to aid the organization in making certain decisions. Such reports may be read primarily by the staff of the organization or by others closely related to the decision-making process.

Reports may be prepared at other times for distribution to the public or to other agencies and institutions. These reports may serve the purpose of informing public opinion or persuading others on matters of public policy.

Whatever the purpose of the short report, its physical appearance and style of presentation should be designed to create a favorable impression on the reader. Even if the report is distributed only within the writer's own unit, an attractive, clear, thorough report will reflect the writer's dedication to his assignment and the pride he takes in his work.

Some guidelines which will assist the trainee in preparation of effective short reports include use of the following:

° A good quality paper;
° Wide and even margins, allowing binding room;
° An accepted standard style of typing;
° A title page;
° A table of contents (for more lengthy reports only);
° A graphic numbering or outlining system, if needed for clarity;
° Graphics and photos to clarify meaning when useful;
° Footnotes, used sparingly, and only when they contribute to the report;
° A bibliography of sources, using a standard citation style.

A discussion of the organization of content for informational reports follows later in this document.

Telegrams and Cables

From time to time messages of special urgency must be sent by public telegraph wires, cables, and radio. With this service, written communications may be exchanged worldwide within minutes at a cost not greatly more than for a letter.

The public-service employee should be familiar with the telegraph service and able to prepare written messages for this
medium. The student should be familiar with the classes of
service available: "full-rate service," "day letter," and
"night letter," since the class of service will affect the
style of writing.

Skill in preparing telegraph messages rests largely on the
writer's ability to summarize. The essential information must
be presented in the fewest possible words. Good messages would
follow these guidelines:

° Omission of articles and prepositions unless essential to
  meaning,

° Use of verb forms of the fewest words,

° Use of single words rather than phrases,

° Omission of unnecessary information and words.

For example:

    "I am taking American Airlines Flight 222 from Chicago
    at 8:15 Wednesday evening and will arrive at Los
    Angeles International Airport at 10:15. I would ap-
    preciate it if you would meet me."

Can be compressed to:

    "Arriving American 222 Los Angeles International
    Wednesday 10:15 PM. Please meet."

The minimum charge on a full-rate telegram is based upon 15
words. The student should develop skill in writing 15-word
summaries in telegraph style.

News Releases

From time to time, the public-service employees may be called
upon to prepare a news release for his agency. Whenever the
activities of the agency are newsworthy or of interest to the
public, the agency has an obligation to report such activities
to the press. The most common means for such reporting is by
using the press release. Most newspapers and broadcasting
stations are initially informed of agencies' activities by
news releases distributed by the agencies themselves. Thus,
the news release is a basic tool for communicating with the
public served by the agency.

The news release is written in news style, with these basic
characteristics:

° Sentences are short and simple.

° Paragraphs are short (one or two sentences) and relate to a single item of information.

° Paragraphs are arranged in *inverted order* - the most important in information appears first.

° The first or *lead* paragraph summarizes the entire story. If the reader went no further, he would have the essential information.

° Subsequent paragraphs provide further details, the most important occurring first.

° Reported information is attributed to sources; that is, the source of the news is reported in the story.

° The expression of the writer's opinions is scrupulously avoided.

° The 5 W's (who, what, why, where, when) are included.

News releases should be typed double spaced on standard 8½ x 11 paper, with generous margins and at least 2" of open space above the lead paragraph. Do not write headlines - that is the editor's job. At the top of the first page of the release include the name of the agency releasing the story and the name and phone number of the person to contact if more information is needed. If the release runs more than one page, end each page with the word "-more-" to indicate that more copy follows. End the release with the symbols "###" to indicate that the copy ends at that point.

Accuracy and physical appearance are essential characteristics of the news release. Typographical errors, or errors of fact, such as misspelled names, lead editors to doubt the reliability of the story. Great care should be taken to assure the accuracy and reliability of a news release.

2. REPORTING ON A TOPIC

At one time or another, most public-service employees will be asked to prepare a report on some topic. Usually the need for the report grows out of some policy decision contemplated by the agency for which full information must be considered. For example:

° Should the agency undertake some new project or service?

° Should working conditions be changed?

° Are new specialists needed on the staff?

° Or should a branch office be opened up?

Or any of a hundred other such decisions which the agency must make from time to time.

When called upon to prepare such a report, the employee should have a model to follow which will guide his collection of information and will help him to prepare an effective and useful report.

As with other forms of written communication, both the physical appearance and content of the report are important to create a favorable impression and to engender confidence. The physical appearance of such reports has been discussed earlier; additional suggestions for reports are given in Unit 3. Basic guidelines follow below for organizing and preparing the content.

Preparation for the Report

What is the Purpose of the Report? The preparer of the report should have clearly in mind why the report is needed:

° What is the decision being contemplated by the agency?

° To what use will the report be put?

Before beginning to prepare the report, the writer should discuss its purpose fully with the decision-making staff to articulate the purpose the report is intended to serve. If the employee is himself initiating the report, it would be well to discuss its purpose with colleagues to assure that its purpose is clear in his own mind.

What Questions Should the Report Answer? Once the purpose of the report is clear, the questions the report must answer may begin to become clear. For example, if the decision faced by the agency is whether or not to offer a new service, questions may be asked such as these:

° What persons would be served by the new service?

° What would the new service cost?

° What new staff would be needed?

° What new equipment and facilities would be needed?

° What alternative ways exist for offering the service?

° How might the new service be administered?

And so on. Unless the purpose of the report is clear, it is difficult to decide what specific questions need to be answered. Once the purpose is clear, these questions can be specified.

Where Can the Relevant Information be Obtained? Once the
questions are clear in the writer's mind, he can identify the
information he will need to answer them. Information may usually be obtained from two general sources:

° *Relevant documents.* Records, publications, and other reports are often useful in locating the information needed
   to answer particular questions. These may be in the files
   of the writer's own agency, in other agencies, or in
   libraries.

° *Personal contacts.* Persons in a position to know the needed
   information may be contacted in person, by phone, or by
   letter. Such contacts are especially important in obtaining
   firsthand accounts of previous experience.

The Text of the Report

What are the Answers to the Questions? Once the relevant information is in hand, the answers to the questions may be assembled.

° What does the information reveal? This activity amounts to
   summarizing the information obtained. It often helps to
   organize this summary around the specific questions asked
   by the report. For example, if the report asks in one part,
   "What are the costs of the new service likely to be?" one
   section of the report should summarize the information gathered to answer this question.

Organizing the Report. The organization of a report into main
and sub-sections depends upon the nature of the report. Reports will differ widely in their organization and treatment.
In general, however, the report should generally follow the
pattern previously discussed. That is, reports which generally
include the following subjects in order will be found to be
clear in their intent and to communicate effectively:

° *Description of problem or purpose.* Example: "One problem
   facing our agency is whether or not we should extend our
   hours of operation to better serve the public. This report is intended to examine the problem and make recommendations."

° *Questions to be answered.* Example: "In examining this problem, answers were sought to the following questions: What
   persons would be served? What would it cost? What staff
   would be needed?"

° *Information sources.* Example: "To answer these questions,
   letters of complaint for the past three years were examined.
   Interviews with clients were conducted by phone and in per-

12

son, phone interviews were conducted with the agency directors in Memphis, Philadelphia, and Chicago."

° *Summary of findings*. Example: "At least 25 percent of the agency's clients would be served better by evening or Saturday service. The costs of operating eight hours of extended service would be negligible, since the service could be provided by rescheduling work assignments. The present staff report they would be inconvenienced by evening and Saturday work assignments."

The Writer's Responsibilities. It is the writer's responsibility to address finally the original purpose of the report. Once the questions have been answered, an informed judgment can be made as to the decision facing the agency. It is at this stage that the writer attempts to draw conclusions from the information he has gathered and summarized. For example, if the original purpose of the report was to help make a decision about whether or not the agency should offer a new service, the writer should draw conclusions from the information and recommend either for or against the new service.

Conclusions and Recommendations. Example: "It appears that operating during extended hours would better serve a significant number of clients. The writer recommends that the agency offer this new service. The present staff should be given temporary assignments to cover the extended hours. As new staff are hired to replace separating persons, they should be hired specifically to cover the extended hours."

3. PERSUASIVE WRITING

Often in life, people are called upon to persuade individuals and groups to adopt ideas believed to be good, or attitudes favorable to ideas thought to be worthwhile or behavior believed to be beneficial. The public service employee may find he must persuade the staff of his own agency, his superiors, the clients of the agency, or the general public in his community.

Persuading others by means of written and other forms of communication is a difficult task and requires much practice. Some principles have emerged from the study of persuasion which may provide some guidelines for developing a model for persuasive writing.

General Guidelines for Writing Persuasively

Know the Credibility of the Source. People are more likely to be persuaded by a message they perceive originates from a trustworthy source. Their trust is enhanced if the source is seen as authoritative, or knowledgeable on the issue discussed in the message. Their trust is increased also if the source appears to have nothing to gain either way, has no vested interest in the final decision. Then, the assertions made in persuasive writing should be backed up by referencing trustworthy and disinterested information sources.

Avoid Overemotional Appeals. Appealing to the common emotions of man - love, hate, fear, sex, etc. - can have a favorable effect on the outcome of a persuasive message. But care should be taken because, if the appeal is too strong, it can lead to a reverse effect. For example, if an agency wanted to persuade the public to get chest X-rays, it would have much greater chance of success if it adopted a positive and helpful attitude rather than trying to frighten them into this action. For instance, appealing mildly to the sense of well-being which accompanies knowledge of one's own good health, instead of shocking the public by showing horror pictures of patients who died from lack of timely X-rays.

Consider the Other Man's Point of View. To persuade another to one's own point of view, should the writer include information and arguments contrary to his own position? Or should he argue only for his own side?

Generally, it depends on where most of the audience stand in the first place. If most of the audience already favor the position being advocated, then the writer will probably do better including only information favorable to his position. However, if the greater part of the audience are likely to oppose this position, then the writer would probably be better off including their arguments also. In this case, he may be helping his cause by rebutting the opposing arguments as he introduces them into the writing.

An example of this technique might occur in arguing for such an idea as a four-day, forty-hour workweek. Thus: "Many people feel that the ten-hour day is too long and that they would arrive home too late for their regular dinner hour. But think! If you have dinner a littler later each night, you'll have a three-day weekend every week. More days free to go fishing, or camping. More days with your wife and children." That is good persuasive writing!

Interpersonal Communications

The important role of interpersonal communication in persuading others - face-to-face and person-to-person communications - has been well documented. Mass mailings or printed messages will likely have less effect than personal letters and conversations between persons already known to each other. In any persuasion campaign the personal touch is very important.

An individual in persuading a large number of persons will likely be more effective if he can organize a letter-writing campaign of persuasive messages written by persons favorable to his position to their friends and acquaintances, than if his campaign is based upon sending out a mass mailing of a printed message.

Conditions for Persuading. In order for an audience of one or many to be persuaded in the manner desired, these conditions must be met:

° the audience must be *exposed* to the message,

° members of the audience must *perceive* the intent of the message,

° they must *remember* the message afterwards,

° each member must *decide* whether or not to adopt the ideas.

Each member of the audience will respond to a message differently. While every person may receive the message, not everyone will read it. Even among those who read it, not everyone will perceive it in the same way. Some will remember it longer than others. Not everyone will decide to adopt the ideas. These effects are called *selective exposure, selective perception, selective retention,* and *selective decision.*

The Persuasion Campaign. How can one counteract these selective effects in persuading others? One thing that is known is that *people tend to be influenced by persuasive messages which they are already predisposed to accept.* This means a person is more likely to persuade people a little than to persuade them a lot.

In planning a persuasion campaign, therefore, the messages should be tailored to the audiences. Success will be more likely if one starts with people who believe *almost* as the writer wants to persuade them to believe - people who are most likely to agree with the position advocated.

The writer also wants to use arguments based on values the particular audience already accepts. For example, in advocating a new teen-age job program, he might argue with busi-ness men that the program will help business; with parents, that it will build character; with teachers, that it is edu-cational; with taxpayers, that it will reduce future taxes; and so on.

The idea is to find some way to make sure that each member of the particular audiences reached can see an advantage for him-self, and for the writer to then tailor the messages for those audiences.

4. INSTRUCTIONAL WRITING

Another task that the public-service employee may expect to face from time to time is the instruction of some other per-son in the performance of a task. This may sometimes involve preparing written instructions to other employees in the unit, or preparing a training manual for new employees.

It may sometimes involve preparing instructional manuals for clients of the unit, such as "How to Apply for a Real Estate License," "How to Bathe your Baby," or "How to Recognize the Symptoms of Heart Disease."

Whatever the purpose or the audience, certain principles of instruction may be applied which will help make more effective these instructional or training communications. These are: *advance organizers, practice, errorless learning,* and *feed-back.*

Advance Organizers

At or near the beginning of an instructional communication, it helps the learner if he is provided with what can be called an "advance organizer." This element of the communication per-forms two functions:

° it provides a framework or "map" for the leader to orga-nize the information he will encounter,

° it helps the learner perceive his purpose in learning the tasks which will follow.

The first paragraphs in this section, for example, serve to-gether as an advance organizer. The trainee is informed that he may be called upon to perform these tasks in his job *(per-ceived purpose)*, and that he will be instructed in advance organizers, practice, errorless learning, and feedback *(frame-work, or "map")*.

Practice

The notion of *practice makes perfect* is a sound instructional principle. When trying to teach someone to perform a task by means of written communication, the writer should build in many opportunities for practicing the task, or parts of it. This built-in practice should be both appropriate and active:

° *Appropriate practice* is practice which is directly related to learning the tasks at hand.

° *Active practice* is practice in actually performing the task at hand or parts of it, rather than simply reading about the task, or thinking about it.

By inserting questions into the text of the communication, by giving practice quizzes, exercises, or field work, one can build into his instructional communication the kind of practice necessary for the reader to readily learn the task.

Errorless Learning

The practice given learners should be easy to do. That is, they should not be asked to practice a task if they are likely to make a lot of mistakes. When a mistake is practiced it is likely to recur again and again, like spelling "demons," which have been spelled wrong so often it's difficult to recall the way they should be spelled. Because it is better to practice a task right from the first, it is important that learners do not make errors in practice.

° One method for encouraging correct practice is to give the reader hints, or *prompts*, to help him practice correctly.

° Another method is to instruct him in a logical sequence a little bit at a time. Don't try to teach everything at once. Break the task down into small parts and teach each part of the task in order. Then give the learner practice in each part of the task before giving him practice in the whole thing.

° A third way of encouraging errorless learning is to build in practice and review throughout the communication. The learner may forget part of the task if the teacher doesn't review it with him from time to time.

Remember, people primarily learn from what they <u>do</u>, so build in to the instructional communication many opportunities for the learner to practice correctly all of the parts of the task required for learning, first separately and then all together.

17

Feedback

The reader, or learner, can't judge how well he is learning the task unless he is informed of it. In a classroom situation, the teacher usually confirms that the learner has been successful, or points out the errors he made, and provides additional instruction. An instructional communication can also help learners in the same way, by providing *feedback* to the learner.

Following practice, the writer should include in his instructional communication information which will let the reader know whether he performed the task correctly. In case he didn't, the writer should also include some further information which will help the reader perform it correctly next time. This feedback, then, performs two functions:

o it helps the learner confirm that his practice was done correctly, and

o it helps him correct his performance of the task in case he made any errors.

Feedback will be most helpful to the learner if it occurs immediately following practice. The learner should be brought to know of his success or his errors just as soon as possible after practice.

STUDENT
LEARNING
ACTIVITIES

o Write "asking" and "answering" letters, and answer a letter of complaint, using the format assigned by the teacher.

o Write memoranda to other "offices" in a fictitious organization. Plan a field trip using only memos to communicate with other students in the class.

o Take minutes of a small group meeting. Or attend a meeting of the school board and take minutes.

o Write a short report on a public service occupation of special interest to you.

o Write a 15-word telegram reserving a single room at a hotel and asking to be picked up at the airport.

o Write a news release announcing a new service offered to the public by your agency.

o Based upon hearing a reading or pretaping of a report, summarize the report in news style.

o View films on effective communication, for example, *Getting the Facts*, *Words that Don't Inform*, and *A Message to No One*.

o For a given problem or purpose, compile a list of specific questions you would need to answer to write a report on the topic.

° For a given list of questions, discuss and compile a list of information sources relevant to the questions.

° As a member of a group, consider the problem of "What field trip should the class take to help students learn how to write an effective news release?" What questions will you need to answer? Where will you obtain your information?

° As a member of a group, gather the information and prepare a short report based on it for presentation to the class.

° Write a report on a problem assigned by your teacher.

° Write a brief persuasive letter to a friend on a given topic. Assume he does not already agree with you. Apply principles of source credibility, emotional appeals, and one or both sides of the issue to persuade him.

° Plan a persuasive campaign to persuade a given segment of your community to take some given action.

° Write a short instructional communication on a verbal learning task assigned by your teacher.

° Write a short instructional communication on a learning task which involves the operation of equipment.

° Try your instructional communications with a fellow student to check for errors during practice.

TEACHER MANAGEMENT ACTIVITIES

° Have students practice letter writing. Assign letters of "asking" and "answering." Read them a letter of complaint and ask them to write an answering letter. Establish common rules of format and style for each assignment. Change the rules from time to time to give practice in several styles.

° Have small groups plan an event, such as a field trip, assigning the various tasks to one another using only memoranda. Evaluate the effectiveness of each group's memo writing by the speed and completeness of their planning.

° Have the class attend a public meeting. Assign each the task of taking the minutes. Evaluate the minutes for brevity and completeness.

° Encourage each student to prepare a short report on a public service occupation of special interest to himself.

° Give the students practice in writing 15-word telegrams.

° Have the students prepare a news release announcing some new service offered to the public, such as "Taxpayers can now obtain help from the Internal Revenue Service in completing their income tax forms as a result of a new service now being offered by the agency."

° Give the students practice in summarizing and writing leads

19

by giving them the facts of a news event and asking them to write a one or two-sentence lead summarizing the significant facts of the event.

° Read a speech or a story. Have students write a summary and a report of the speech or story in news style.

° Show films on effective communication, for example, *Getting the Facts, Words that Don't Inform,* and *A Message to No One.*

° State a general problem and have each student prepare a list of the specific questions implied by the problem.

° State a list of specific questions and discuss with the class the sources of information which might bear upon each of the questions.

° Have small groups consider and write short reports jointly on the general problem, "What field trip should the class take to help students learn how to write an effective news release?" Have each group identify the specific questions to be answered, with sources for needed information.

° Have each student identify and prepare a short report on a general problem of interest.

° Assign students to work in groups of three or four to draft a letter to a friend to persuade him to make a contribution to establish a new city art museum.

° Assign the students to groups of five or six, each group to map out a persuasive campaign on a given topic. Some topics are "Give Blood," "Get Chest X-Ray," "Quit Smoking," "Don't Litter," "Inspect Your House Wiring," etc.

° Have each student identify a simple verbal learning task and prepare an instructional communication to teach that task to another student not familiar with the task.

° Have each student prepare an instructional manual designed to train someone to operate some simple piece of equipment, such as an adding machine, a slide projector, a tape recorder, or something of similar complexity.

° Have each student try his instructional communication out on another student, unfamiliar with the task. He should observe the activities and responses of the trial student to identify errors made in practice. He should revise the communication, adding practice, review, and prompts wherever needed to reduce errors in practice.

EVALUATION QUESTIONS

Written Communications

1. **Which type of letter would be correct for a public service worker to send:**
   A. A letter containing erasures
   B. A letter reflecting goodwill
   C. A rude letter
   D. An impersonal letter

2. **Memos usually leave out:**
   A. Complimentary closings
   B. The name of the sender
   C. The name of the addressee
   D. The date the memo was sent

3. **A good business letter would not contain:**
   A. Short, simple words, sentences, and paragraphs
   B. Information contained in the letter being answered
   C. Concrete nouns and active verbs
   D. Orderly placed paragraphs

4. **In writing business letters it is important to:**
   A. Use a conversational tone
   B. Use a hard, cold tone
   C. Use abstract words
   D. Use a passive tone

5. **Messages between departments in an agency are usually sent by:**
   A. Letter
   B. Memo
   C. Telegram
   D. Long reports

6. **Repetitive work can be simplified by the use of:**
   A. Memos
   B. Telegrams
   C. Forms
   D. Reports

7. **In filling out forms and applications, it is important to be:**
   A. Legible
   B. Complete
   C. Accurate
   D. All of the above

21

8. Memos should be:
   A. Clear   ————
   B. Brief ————
   C. Complete ————
   D. All of the above ————

9. Minutes of meetings should not include:
   A. The opinions of the recorder ————
   B. The approval of previous minutes ————
   C. The corrections of previous minutes ————
   D. The voting members present ————

10. Reports are written by public service workers to:
   A. Assemble information in one place ————
   B. Aid the organization in making decisions ————
   C. Inform the public and other agencies ————
   D. All of the above ————

11. News releases should include:
   A. A lead paragraph summarizing the story ————
   B. Long paragraphs about many topics ————
   C. The writer's opinion ————
   D. All of the above ————

12. Readers of news releases and reports are influenced by the:
   A. Content of the material ————
   B. Accuracy of the material ————
   C. Physical appearance of the material ————
   D. All of the above ————

13. The contents of a report should not include:
   A. A description of the problem ————
   B. The questions to be answered ————
   C. Unimportant information ————
   D. A summary of findings ————

14. People tend to be influenced easier if:
   A. They can see something in the position that would be advantageous to them ————
   C. They are almost ready to agree anyhow ————
   C. The appeal to the emotions is not overly strong ————
   D. All of the above ————

————

Answer Key

1. B	4. A	7. D	10. D	13. C
2. A	5. B	8. D	11. A	14. D
3. B	6. C	9. A	12. D	

————

PROOFREADING

C O N T E N T S

PROOFREADING

PROOFREADER'S MARKS

⊙	INSERT PERIOD		⊐	INDENT 1 EM
⋀	INSERT COMMA		⊐⊐	INDENT 2 EMS
;	INSERT COLON		¶	PARAGRAPH
?	INSERT QUESTION MARK		no ¶	NO PARAGRAPH
!	INSERT EXCLAMATION MARK		tr	TRANSPOSE-USED IN MARGIN
=/	INSERT HYPHEN		∿	TRANSPOSE-USED IN TEXT
⋁	INSERT APOSTROPHE		sp	SPELL OUT
⋁ ⋁	INSERT QUOTATION MARKS		ital	ITALIC-USED IN MARGIN
⼍	INSERT 1-EN DASH		——	ITALIC-USED IN TEXT
⼍	INSERT 1-EM DASH		b.f.	BOLDFACE-USED IN MARGIN
#	INSERT SPACE		⌇	BOLDFACE-USED IN TEXT
ld>	INSERT LEAD		s.c.	SMALL CAPS-USED IN MARGIN
shill	INSERT VIRGULE		=	SMALL CAPS-USED IN TEXT
V	SUPERIOR		rom.	ROMAN TYPE
⋀	INFERIOR		Caps.	CAPS-USED IN MARGIN
(/)	PARENTHESES		≡	CAPS-USED IN TEXT
[/]	BRACKETS		l.c.	LOWER CASE-USED IN MARGIN

/ LOWER CASE-USED IN TEXT

W.f. WRONG FONT

⌒ CLOSE UP

ℱ DELETE

ℱ CLOSE UP AND DELETE

𝟡 CORRECT THE POSITION

⌐ MOVE RIGHT

⌐ MOVE LEFT

⊓ MOVE UP

⊔ MOVE DOWN

‖ ALINE VERTICALLY

⹀ ALINE HORIZONTALLY

⊐⊏ CENTER HORIZONTALLY

⨅ CENTER VERTICALLY

⌣ PUSH DOWN SPACE

⌒ USE LIGATURE

eq.# EQUALIZE SPACE-USED IN MARGIN

√∫√ EQUALIZE SPACE-USED IN TEXT

√ DECREASE SPACE

stet. LET IT STAND-USED IN MARGIN

.... LET IT STAND-USED IN TEXT

ⓧ DIRTY OR BROKEN LETTER

run over CARRY OVER TO NEXT LINE

run back CARRY BACK TO PRECEDING LINE

Copy out SOMETHING OMITTED-SEE COPY

Qu? (?) QUESTION TO AUTHOR

∧ CARET-GENERAL INDICATOR USED TO MARK EXACT POSITION OF
ERROR IN TEXT

; INSERT SEMICOLON

C+SC CAPS & SMALL CAPS-USED IN MARGIN

= CAPS & SMALL CAPS-USED IN TEXT

It does not appear that the earliest printers had
any method of correcting errors before the form
was on the press. The learned The learned cor-
rectors of the first two centuries of printing were
notproofreaders in our sense, they were rather
what we should term office editors. Their labors
were chiefly to see that the proof corresponded to
the copy, but that the printed page was correct
in its Latinity, that the words were there, and
that the sense was right. They cared but little
about orthography, bad letters or purely printers'
errors, and when the text seemed to them wrong
they consulted fresh authorities or altered it on
their own responsibility. Good proofs in the
modern sense, were impossible until professional
readers were employed, men who had first a
printer's education, and then spent many years
in the correction of proof. The orthography of
English, which for the past century has under
gone little change, was very fluctuating until after
the publication of Johnson's Dictionary, and capi-
tals, which have been used with considerable reg-
ularity for the past 80 years, were previously used
on the miss or hit plan. The approach to regu-

larity, so far as we have may be attributed to the growth of a class of professional proofreaders, and it is to them that we owe the correctness of modern printing. More errors have been found in the Bible than in any other one work. For many generations it was frequently the case that Bibles were brought out stealthily, from fear of governmental interference. They were frequently printed from imperfect texts, and were often modified to meet the views of those who published them. The story is related that a certain woman in Germany, who was the wife of a printer, and who had become disgusted with the continual assertions of the *superiority* of man over woman which she had heard, hurried into the composing room while her husband was at supper and altered a sentence in the Bible, which he was printing, so that it read Narr instead of Herr, thus making the verse read "And he shall be thy fool" instead of "And he shall be thy lord." The word not was omitted by Barker, the King's printer in England in 1632, in printing the seventh commandment. He was fined £3,000 on this account.

ANSWER SHEET

TEST NO. _____ PART _____ TITLE OF POSITION _____

PLACE OF EXAMINATION _____ DATE_____

(CITY OR TOWN) (STATE)

RATING

USE THE SPECIAL PENCIL. MAKE GLOSSY BLACK MARKS.

A B C D E — repeated columns for questions 1–10, 26–35, 51–60, 76–85, 101–110

1 2 3 4 5 6 7 8 9 10
26 27 28 29 30 31 32 33 34 35
51 52 53 54 55 56 57 58 59 60
76 77 78 79 80 81 82 83 84 85
101 102 103 104 105 106 107 108 109 110

Make only ONE mark for each answer. Additional and stray marks may be counted as mistakes. In making corrections, erase errors COMPLETELY.

A B C D E — repeated columns for questions 11–25, 36–50, 61–75, 86–100, 111–125

11 12 13 14 15 16 17 18 19 20 21 22 23 24 25
36 37 38 39 40 41 42 43 44 45 46 47 48 49 50
61 62 63 64 65 66 67 68 69 70 71 72 73 74 75
86 87 88 89 90 91 92 93 94 95 96 97 98 99 100
111 112 113 114 115 116 117 118 119 120 121 122 123 124 125

ANSWER SHEET

WITHDRAWN
WITHDRAWN

TEST NO. _____ PART _____ TITLE OF POSITION _____

PLACE OF EXAMINATION _____ DATE_____

(CITY OR TOWN)　　　　　　　　　　　　　　(STATE)

RATING

USE THE SPECIAL PENCIL. MAKE GLOSSY BLACK MARKS.

1 A B C D E   26 A B C D E   51 A B C D E   76 A B C D E   101 A B C D E
2 A B C D E   27 A B C D E   52 A B C D E   77 A B C D E   102 A B C D E
3 A B C D E   28 A B C D E   53 A B C D E   78 A B C D E   103 A B C D E
4 A B C D E   29 A B C D E   54 A B C D E   79 A B C D E   104 A B C D E
5 A B C D E   30 A B C D E   55 A B C D E   80 A B C D E   105 A B C D E
6 A B C D E   31 A B C D E   56 A B C D E   81 A B C D E   106 A B C D E
7 A B C D E   32 A B C D E   57 A B C D E   82 A B C D E   107 A B C D E
8 A B C D E   33 A B C D E   58 A B C D E   83 A B C D E   108 A B C D E
9 A B C D E   34 A B C D E   59 A B C D E   84 A B C D E   109 A B C D E
10 A B C D E 35 A B C D E   60 A B C D E   85 A B C D E   110 A B C D E

Make only ONE mark for each answer. Additional and stray marks may be
counted as mistakes. In making corrections, erase errors COMPLETELY.

11 A B C D E 36 A B C D E   61 A B C D E   86 A B C D E   111 A B C D E
12 A B C D E 37 A B C D E   62 A B C D E   87 A B C D E   112 A B C D E
13 A B C D E 38 A B C D E   63 A B C D E   88 A B C D E   113 A B C D E
14 A B C D E 39 A B C D E   64 A B C D E   89 A B C D E   114 A B C D E
15 A B C D E 40 A B C D E   65 A B C D E   90 A B C D E   115 A B C D E
16 A B C D E 41 A B C D E   66 A B C D E   91 A B C D E   116 A B C D E
17 A B C D E 42 A B C D E   67 A B C D E   92 A B C D E   117 A B C D E
18 A B C D E 43 A B C D E   68 A B C D E   93 A B C D E   118 A B C D E
19 A B C D E 44 A B C D E   69 A B C D E   94 A B C D E   119 A B C D E
20 A B C D E 45 A B C D E   70 A B C D E   95 A B C D E   120 A B C D E
21 A B C D E 46 A B C D E   71 A B C D E   96 A B C D E   121 A B C D E
22 A B C D E 47 A B C D E   72 A B C D E   97 A B C D E   122 A B C D E
23 A B C D E 48 A B C D E   73 A B C D E   98 A B C D E   123 A B C D E
24 A B C D E 49 A B C D E   74 A B C D E   99 A B C D E   124 A B C D E
25 A B C D E 50 A B C D E   75 A B C D E 100 A B C D E   125 A B C D E